AMERICA'S NATIONAL PARKS

ACADIA
NATIONAL PARK

ADVENTURE, EXPLORE, DISCOVER

AMY GRAHAM

MyReportLinks.com Books
an imprint of
 Enslow Publishers, Inc.
Box 398, 40 Industrial Road
Berkeley Heights, NJ 07922
USA

MyReportLinks.com Books, an imprint of Enslow Publishers, Inc. MyReportLinks®
is a registered trademark of Enslow Publishers, Inc.

Library of Congress Cataloging-in-Publication Data

Graham, Amy.
  Acadia National Park : adventure, explore, discover / Amy Graham.
    p. cm. — (America's national parks)
  Includes bibliographical references and index.
  Audience: Grades 4-6.
  ISBN-13: 978-1-59845-090-3 (hardcover)
  ISBN-10: 1-59845-090-5 (hardcover)
  1. Acadia National Park (Me.)—Juvenile literature. I. Title.
  F27.M9G73 2008
  974.1'45—dc22

                        2007000952

Printed in the United States of America

10 9 8 7 6 5 4 3 2 1

To Our Readers:
Through the purchase of this book, you and your library gain access to the Report Links that specifically back up this book.
The Publisher will provide access to the Report Links that back up this book and will keep these Report Links up to date on **www.myreportlinks.com** for five years from the book's first publication date.
We have done our best to make sure all Internet addresses in this book were active and appropriate when we went to press. However, the author and the Publisher have no control over, and assume no liability for, the material available on those Internet sites or on other Web sites they may link to.
The usage of the MyReportLinks.com Books Web site is subject to the terms and conditions stated on the Usage Policy Statement on **www.myreportlinks.com**.
A password may be required to access the Report Links that back up this book. The password is found on the bottom of page 4 of this book.
Any comments or suggestions can be sent by e-mail to comments@myreportlinks.com or to the address on the back cover.

♻ Enslow Publishers, Inc., is committed to printing our books on recycled paper. The paper in every book contains 10% to 30% post-consumer waste (PCW). The cover board on the outside of each book contains 100% PCW. Our goal is to do our part to help young people and the environment too!

Photo Credits: AP/ Wide World Photos, pp. 54–55; Abbe Museum, p. 28; americanparknetwork.com, p. 10; © Corel Corporation, pp. 52–53, 60–61, 81; The Ecological Society of America (ESA), p. 91; Friends of Acadia, p. 95; GORPcom, p. 46; Handsontheland.org, p. 90; Greg A. Hartford (Acadia WS), p. 58; Hazecam.net, p. 87; The Herbert Hoover Presidential Library and Museum, p. 49; Hillclimb Media, p. 104; istockphoto.com: pp. 3, 12–13 (Ariel Maor), 16–17 (Carl Kelliher), 6 (Bar Harbor) & 22–23 (David Cannings-Bushell), 26–27 (Andrea Pelletier), 56–57 (Michael Westhoff), 72 (Paul Tessier), 84–85 (Keith Webber Jr.), 7 (bicyclist) & 102–103 (Jerry Whaley); Leave No Trace Center for Outdoor Ethics, p. 92; Library of Congress, pp. 31, 45, 47, 48; Maine.gov, p. 80; The Maine Wolf Coalition, p. 78; The Mariners' Museum, pp. 29, 30; MyReportLinks.com Books, p. 4; National Geographic, p. 67; National Park Service/Enslow Publishers, Inc., p. 5; National Park Service, pp. 8–9 (Todd Edgar), 21, 69, 70–71 (Dave Smith), 100; National Parks Conservation Association, pp. 86, 88; Natural Resources Council of Maine, p. 73; PBS, p. 36; The Rockefeller Archive Center, p. 44; shutterstock.com, pp. 6 (top tidal pool photo, Bass Harbor Light), 20 (Jeff Schultes), 32–33, 42–43 (Jerry Whaley), 6 (loon) & 64 (Sebastien Gauthier), 98, 108–109, 112–113 (Gary Detonnancourt); US-Parks.com, p. 66; U.S. Fish & Wildlife Service, pp. 7 (deer), 79; U.S. Geological Survey/ Northern Prairie Wildlife Research Center, p. 74; The Woodlawn Museum, p. 40.

Cover Photo and Description: © Greg A. Hartford: Sailboat on Somes Sound, Mount Desert Island.

CONTENTS

MyReportLinks.com Books
Great Books, Great Links, Great for Research!

The Internet sites featured in this book can save you hours of research time. These Internet sites—we call them **"Report Links"**—are constantly changing, but we keep them up to date on our Web site.

When you see this "Approved Web Site" logo, you will know that we are directing you to a great Internet site that will help you with your research.

Give it a try! Type **http://www.myreportlinks.com** into your browser, click on the series title and enter the password, then click on the book title, and scroll down to the Report Links listed for this book.

The Report Links will bring you to great source documents, photographs, and illustrations. MyReportLinks.com Books save you time, feature Report Links that are kept up to date, and make report writing easier than ever! A complete listing of the Report Links can be found on pages 116–117 at the back of the book.

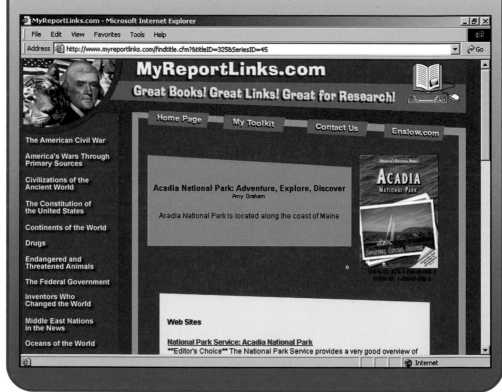

Please see "To Our Readers" on the copyright page for important information about this book, the MyReportLinks.com Web site, and the Report Links that back up this book.

Please enter **ANP1571** if asked for a password.

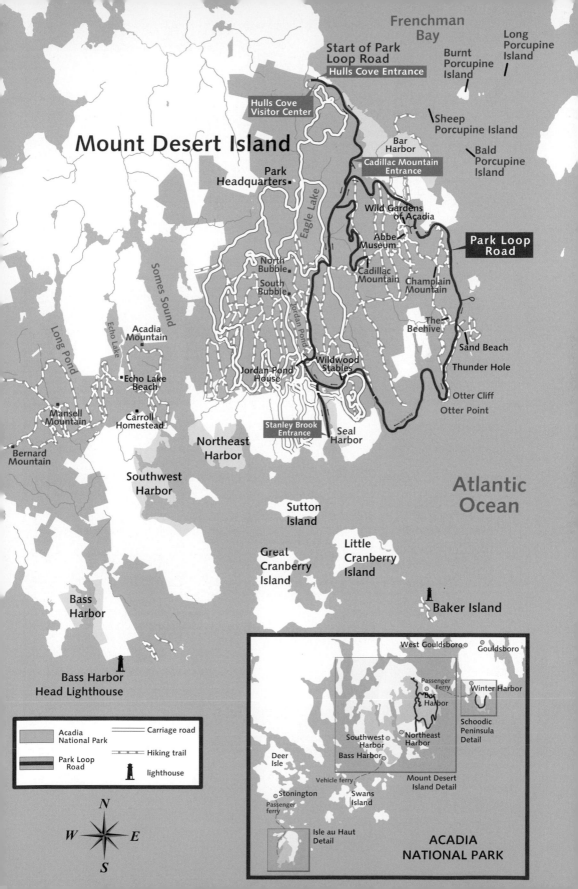

🍁 Acadia National Park is the only national park in the northeastern United States.

🍁 Acadia was the first national park established east of the Mississippi.

🍁 Acadia is one of the top ten most visited national parks in America.

🍁 More than 2 million people visit Acadia National Park each year.

🍁 The park encompasses more than forty-five thousand acres.

🍁 The heart of Acadia National Park is Mount Desert Island, the largest island off the coast of the state of Maine. Mount Desert Island is reached by crossing a short bridge from the mainland, and has twenty-eight freshwater lakes and ponds.

🍁 Cadillac Mountain on Mount Desert Island is the highest point on America's East Coast at 1,530 feet. From early October to early March, Cadillac Mountain gets the first rays of sunlight to hit the United States each morning.

🍁 The Wabanaki Indians who once lived here called the island Pemetic, or the sloping land.

🍁 Schoodic Point, a nearby peninsula on the mainland, has been part of Acadia National Park since 1929.

🍁 Acadia also includes much of Isle au Haut, a smaller island to the southwest of Mount Desert Island. Isle au Haut is not accessible from Mount Desert Island.

🍁 A mail boat goes to Isle au Haut each day from the town of Stonington, Maine.

🍁 Stonington is two hours away from Mount Desert Island by car.

🍁 When it first became a national park in 1919, Acadia had a different name. It was called Lafayette National Park. The park's name was changed from Lafayette to Acadia in 1929.

❀ Forty-five miles of gravel carriage roads, open only to foot, bicycle, and horse traffic, wind through the park.

❀ The park boasts one hundred and twenty-five miles of hiking trails.

❀ There are twenty-six mountains in Acadia National Park. They are part of an ancient mountain chain.

❀ Somes Sound, a five-mile-long finger of the ocean that nearly splits Mount Desert Island in two, is the only fjord on the Atlantic Coast of the United States.

❀ Acadia is the only national park that the national government did not have to purchase. The land was donated, much of it by wealthy patron John D. Rockefeller, Jr.

❀ The wildfire of 1947 destroyed seventeen thousand acres on Mount Desert Island and more than sixty summer residences.

❀ French explorer Samuel de Champlain named the island "Isle des Monts Deserts," or "island of bare mountains" after spotting the barren mountain tops in 1604. Today, many people still pronounce the island's name Mount "Dessert," in the French fashion.

❀ Peregrine falcons, extinct in the park at one time, have been successfully reintroduced to Acadia.

❀ The Hulls Cove Visitor Center, open from mid-April through October, offers a fifteen-minute orientation film and three-dimensional map of the island, as well as assistance from park rangers to plan out a visit.

❀ Large parts of the Park Loop Road are closed down for the winter season.

❀ Even in the summer months, the Atlantic Ocean off the coast of Maine does not get much warmer than fifty-five degrees (Fahrenheit).

Chapter

1

View of the mountains of Mount Desert Island taken from a vantage point on nearby Baker Island.

A Trip to Acadia National Park

When they saw the mountains, the family knew they were drawing near Acadia National Park. For the last few hours, they had meandered along the coast of Maine. Their route had taken them through small fishing villages. They had seen rocky fields of low bush blueberries. Now the rounded mountains of Mount Desert Island rose up in front of them. They were quite different from anything the family had yet seen.

"Are you sure these are mountains, Mom? They look more like hills," one of the kids piped up from the backseat. It was true: the mountains were not very tall. They were not jagged or craggy, but smooth and worn. The mother explained that they were the remains of an ancient chain of granite mountains. About fifteen thousand years ago, a mile-thick ice sheet flowed over this land. It picked up rocks as it went. The rocks and ice scraped across the land, scouring the mountains. The ice sheet was so heavy that it had pressed the mountains down into the crust of the earth. It carved out valleys and lake beds.

Now the mountains looked like big, slumbering tortoises. Their tops were bald. Seen from a distance, the peaks appeared to stand in a proud line. As they drew closer, the family could see that the mountains rose up all over the large island.

It was a lovely late summer day. The sun was out and the sky was clear. If they had arrived in a bank of fog, the visitors might never have known there were mountains at all.

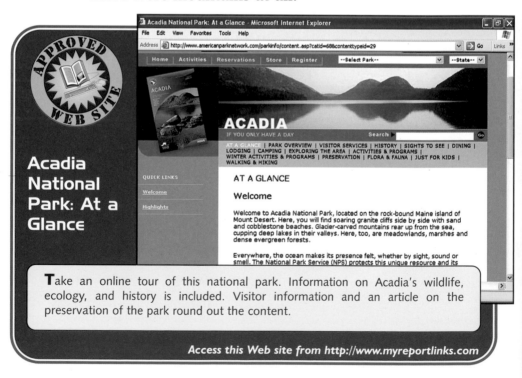

Take an online tour of this national park. Information on Acadia's wildlife, ecology, and history is included. Visitor information and an article on the preservation of the park round out the content.

Access this Web site from http://www.myreportlinks.com

Fog is common in Acadia, especially in the summer months. Warm summer air blows over the cold Atlantic Ocean. The air picks up water and forms a low-lying cloud that settles over the island. Some fogs are so thick and damp, it is impossible to see more than a few feet. The locals call this a "pea soup" fog, and it is as murky as a bowl of that heavy soup.

Fog may block the views, but it gives people a different kind of adventure. Not only is it hard to see, it is hard to hear, too. The fog muffles sounds. It makes it difficult to get one's bearings. Then suddenly the sun shines through and the fog lifts, as quickly as it came.

CROSSING TO MOUNT DESERT ISLAND

Leaving the mainland, the family crossed a bridge that spanned a slender channel of water called the Narrows. Finally, they were on Mount Desert Island. Everyone let out a cheer. A sign welcomed them to Acadia National Park. Two thirds of the large island belongs to the park.

After a quick stop at the Hull's Cove Visitor Center, the family set out to explore the island. It was already mid-afternoon. They had piled into the car early that morning, before the sun was even up. Now they were ready to stretch their legs and see the sights.

The only sandy beach on Mount Desert Island, Sand Beach is a highlight for many visitors to Acadia National Park.

They followed the Park Loop Road to the first attraction: Sand Beach. The visitors were happy to leave their car in the parking lot. A cold wind whipped through everyone's hair, and they reached for their jackets. The family followed the granite stairs down to the beach. By the time they reached the bottom, the large parking lot was out of sight. It was as if they had stepped through a door into a different world. The air fell still; the chilly wind was gone. A large sand beach spread out in front of them. Steep cliffs covered with a dark forest of pointy spruce trees rose up on either side of the cove.

Seagulls soared overhead, calling to one another with raspy voices. A lone crow landed briefly on the sand. It hopped about for a moment, and then took off, flapping its black wings. Ocean waves rolled onto the beach one after another in a steady rhythm. The air was sunny and warm. The children shed their jackets and took off at a run. Their parents followed behind, enjoying the view of the sea.

At the mouth of the cove, there was one rocky ledge rising up out of the water. Beyond that, the Atlantic Ocean stretched on as far as they could see. They could see a lone sailboat gliding along, its white sails puffed out full with wind.

The tide was out. At the top of the beach, dried black seaweed and gulls' feathers decorated the sand. A fence blocked off the fragile sand dunes. Behind the dunes, they could see a mound or hill of rock called the Beehive. Long ago the ice had worn grooves into the hillside. Now it truly did resemble a beehive. They could see people climbing hand over hand up the steep cliffs far beyond. These were hikers following one of the park's most popular trails. Near the top of the Beehive, there is a small pond called the Bowl. It is a great place to cool off after a tough hike. The children vowed they would make the climb during their stay in Acadia.

THE ANOMALY OF THE SANDY BEACH

The sandy beach was beautiful, but it looked a bit out of place. All along the east coast of Maine, the ocean waves meet a rocky shore. In places, dark forests cover the land all the way down to where the Atlantic Ocean crashes against bare cliffs.

There are also many cobblestone beaches. A cobblestone beach looks like a big pile of rocks. The rocks are rounded, with edges worn smooth by the constant rubbing and rolling in water. The rocks clink and clatter together as the undertow pulls the water back out to sea.

But here was a mysterious sandy beach. The visitors were curious. Why was this beach the only sandy one on the island? A park ranger wearing a green and gray uniform and a broadbrimmed hat was happy to explain. It had to do with how the deep cove is so protected. The sand is able to collect there rather than wash away, she said.

The ranger asked them if they had felt the sand yet. They reached down to touch it with their fingers. It felt gritty. She told them that the sand had an unusually high content of shell fragments. Most sand is made up of little fragments of rock. At this beach, the sand was made up of tiny pieces of granite rock. The granite was mixed with pieces of the shells of millions of sea animals. The children looked at each other in amazement.

Though their swimsuits were packed away in the trunk of the car, the children couldn't resist testing the water. They waded in and quickly ran back out, laughing and screeching. Even at the height of summer, the ocean water was frigid. The ocean waters off the coast of Maine never get much warmer than 55°F (about 13°C). Not that the cold temperatures stop people from swimming here, for there is no better way to cool down on a hot summer's day.

The tide was starting to rise. "This would be a good time to check out Thunder Hole," advised the park

ranger. Reluctantly, the children returned to the car. They made plans to return to Sand Beach with their bathing suits and a picnic lunch the next day.

THE MYSTERY OF THUNDER HOLE

They were at Thunder Hole in no time, since it was just a mile down the Park Loop Road. Right away, they heard a loud boom and felt the rock under their feet reverberate. The children broke out in a run to see what was making the noise. They slowed when they reached a stairway leading down toward the shore. There was quite a crowd gathered around a large chasm in the cliff. An

Waves crash into the rocks with a loud booming sound at Thunder Hole.

incoming wave surged and flooded into the cave. When it broke, it sprayed salt water high in the air, soaking some tourists who were standing a bit too close.

Boom! There was that loud sound again. A sign explained where the sound came from. Over the years, the ocean had worn away at a weak spot in the rock. It formed a cave, part of which was underwater. When waves rushed into the cave, they trapped air inside. When the pressure grew too strong, the air rushed out with a loud booming sound. The children could hear another sound—the rumbling of their stomachs! They'd been having so much fun, they'd forgotten to eat. "I have a treat in store for you," their father said. "But first, let's take a look at Otter Cliffs."

⊜OTTER CLIFFS

They followed the twists and turns of the shoreline on the Park Loop Road. On their left, they saw the Otter Cliffs. A wall of granite rose straight out of the ocean, 110 feet into the air. "Will we see the otters?" asked one of the kids. "Not likely," her mother answered. "Sea otters don't live in the Atlantic Ocean."

"So, what are the cliffs named after?" asked the father, puzzled.

"Probably the sea mink," his wife replied. "It was an ocean animal that lived in this area. People hunted them for their fur. It is a sad story. The hunters went too far. The sea minks have been extinct for more than a hundred years."[1] They all looked out the window as the road took a turn inland.

→ Jordan Pond and the Bubbles

Before long the family was sitting at a table, hungrily eyeing their food. There were rich popovers, a tub of butter, and another tub filled to the brim with strawberry jam. This was no ordinary restaurant. The table sat on a grassy lawn. In front of them was a scenic view.

The waters of Jordan Pond gently lapped the shore. Bumpy mountains rose up on the other side of the water. These mountains were called North and South Bubbles. Behind the family was the Jordan Pond Tea House. A teahouse had been on this site for over a century. After they had eaten, they explored the nature trail around the pond. Tired out, everyone climbed back in the car.

→ Bubble Rock

The road took them along the side of the pond. Looking up at South Bubble Mountain, they saw a huge boulder that sat at a tilt on the rocky mountaintop. It seemed a bit precarious. If someone leaned on it, would it come crashing down the mountainside? They looked the rock up in a

Jordan Pond is shown with the backdrop of the nearby mountains, the North and South Bubbles.

guidebook. The boulder was named Bubble Rock. It was different from other rocks on the island. It was not from the island, but was moved here from its home—thirty miles to the north.

What was strong enough to move this huge rock such a distance? And what left it here, on top of a mountain? It was the same ice sheet that thousands of years ago scraped the mountains bare. The ice swept the rock up and carried it along. When the ice began to melt, it set the rock down. Bubble Rock is a good example of what geologists call a glacial erratic.[2]

This site presented by the National Park Service's Geological Resources Division helps to explain the park's geological structure in **Geology Fieldnotes: Acadia National Park.** Information about soil characteristics, estuaries, bedrock foundations, glaciers, and shore patterns is included here, along with geologic maps and data.

A view of Bar Harbor shown from the summit of Cadillac Mountain.

→VIEW FROM THE TOP

The day was drawing to a close. The sun had sunk low in the sky, and its rays tinged a few clouds a bright shade of crimson. It looked as though they would enjoy a colorful sunset this evening. The visitors decided to end their first day in Acadia with a view from the top of Cadillac Mountain. The summit of Cadillac is the highest spot on the island. They were surprised to read that Cadillac is also the highest spot on the entire East Coast of North America.

A road snaked back and forth up the mountain. Their car crept slowly to the top, and the family admired the views along the way. At the summit, they parked the car and set out to explore. There were no trees, and there was very little soil for a tree to take root in. The mountaintop was too exposed to the rain and the wind. In a few pro-tected places, small plants grew low to the ground. Following a trail, the children clambered over the bare slabs of pink granite. The rock really did look a rosy shade of pink, speckled with gray.

From the summit of Cadillac, all of Acadia lay at their feet. They could see in every direction. The Atlantic Ocean was vast. It went on and on until, in the far distance, it met up with the sky. Small islands, both rocky and wooded, dotted the nearby bays. "Maybe we can get up early one morning. I would like to come back up here to see a sunrise," said the mother. "People say that the top of Cadillac Mountain is the first place in the nation to see the sun come up."

Maine is the most eastern state, she explained. When the sun rises in the east each morning, the Down East coast of Maine is first to greet the sun. Because Cadillac is the highest spot on the Maine coast, at certain times of the year (from early October through early March) the sun hits here before anywhere else.

"Why is this part of the Maine coast called *Down* East?" asked one of the kids. "I understand why they call it east. But why *Down* East?"

"I know the answer to that," said his father. "Originally it was a sailing term. Ships coming here from the ports to the south, such as Boston or Portland, sailed east along the coast. The prevailing winds were at their backs, helping them along. In other words, they sailed downwind, and so they called it sailing down east. The name stuck, and today "Down East" refers to the eastern coast of Maine."

Someone stifled a big yawn. It was time for bed. On the way to the hotel, everyone thought about what they had seen that day. It had been fun. They thought about the adventures they would have in Acadia over the next week.

Chapter 2

Bubble Pond, a short distance northeast of Jordan Pond, is bordered by one of the carriage roads.

History of Mount Desert Island

People have lived on the coast of Maine for the last five thousand years. Broken shards of pottery and arrowheads found in Maine date back that far. Human bones have also been unearthed. The graves with these remains contained bright red ocher stain mix. This red paint may have been part of a burial ceremony. The Red Paint people were the early ancestors of the American Indian tribes of Maine.[1]

➡ PEMETIC: LAND OF THE SLOPING MOUNTAINS

Hundreds of years ago, American Indians lived on Mount Desert Island. They called it Pemetic, which means "the sloping land."

They spent the winter months on the island. At that time of year, the inland lakes and rivers froze solid. Deep snow covered the ground, making it difficult to hunt.

On the coast, though, food was more plentiful. Huge flocks of arctic seabirds wintered on the

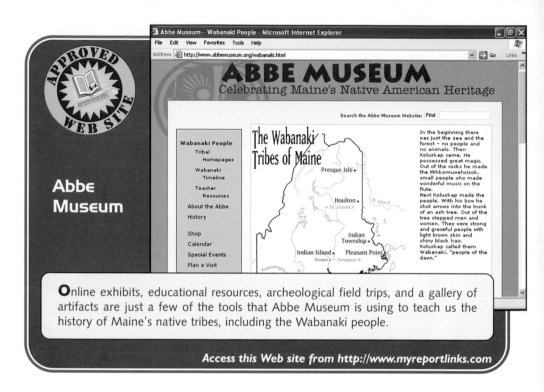

Online exhibits, educational resources, archeological field trips, and a gallery of artifacts are just a few of the tools that Abbe Museum is using to teach us the history of Maine's native tribes, including the Wabanaki people.

Access this Web site from http://www.myreportlinks.com

coast of Maine. Cod, a kind of cold-water fish, were easy to catch in traps called weirs. The people built canoes from the white papery bark of birch trees and paddled them out onto the ocean, where they could fish and hunt near the water's edge. The women harvested shellfish, such as mussels, clams, and whelks. The inedible shells were dumped in big piles. These shell piles, called middens, still remain today.

Two different tribes lived on Mount Desert Island. They were the Penobscot and the Passamaquoddy. Both tribes were part of a larger nation, the Wabanaki. Their name means *people of the dawn.* They lived far to the east of the mainland, where the sun first rises.

At one time, there were as many as thirty-two thousand American Wabanaki Indians.[2] Then people from Europe came to explore the region. They set up camp on the islands offshore. They brought fish and feathers back to Europe, met the Wabanaki, and traded with them.

Unfortunately, they also brought diseases with them from the Old World. Smallpox and influenza were new to the Wabanaki. In 1616, a great plague broke out, spreading like wildfire. A few years later, an estimated three out of every four Wabanaki had died.[3]

The Mariners' Museum tells the story of Giovanni da Verrazzano's voyages in the sixteenth century. Information about the type of ship he sailed on his expeditions and details of routes he took is on this Web site.

Access this Web site from http://www.myreportlinks.com

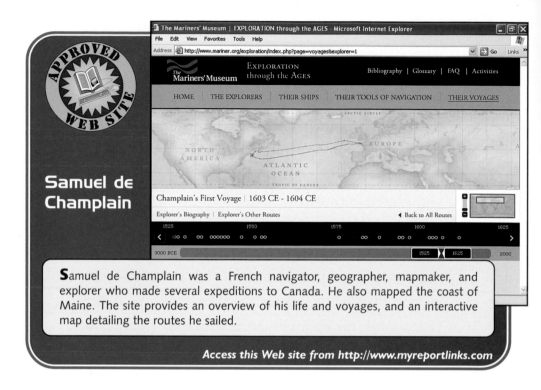

The Mariners' Museum | EXPLORATION through the AGES - Microsoft Internet Explorer

File   Edit   View   Favorites   Tools   Help

Address   http://www.mariner.org/exploration/index.php?page=voyages&explorer=1   Go   Links

EXPLORATION
through the AGES

The Mariners' Museum

Bibliography | Glossary | FAQ | Activities

HOME   THE EXPLORERS   THEIR SHIPS   THEIR TOOLS OF NAVIGATION   THEIR VOYAGES

Champlain's First Voyage | 1603 CE - 1604 CE

Explorer's Biography | Explorer's Other Routes   ◀ Back to All Routes

Samuel de Champlain

Samuel de Champlain was a French navigator, geographer, mapmaker, and explorer who made several expeditions to Canada. He also mapped the coast of Maine. The site provides an overview of his life and voyages, and an interactive map detailing the routes he sailed.

Access this Web site from http://www.myreportlinks.com

➡ EXPLORERS FROM EUROPE

Who was the first European to see Mount Desert Island? No one is sure. It may have been Giovanni da Verrazzano. He was an Italian sea captain for the country of France and was one of the first Europeans to chart the New World.

In 1524, he sailed along the East Coast of North America. He made note of the large islands of Mount Desert, Manhattan, and Nantucket on his maps. It was Verrazzano who first named the coast "Acadia." Some say he based this name on a Wabanaki word.[4] Others claim that the rocky cliffs reminded him of a place from Greek mythology.[5]

In 1604, a crew of Frenchman came to claim *l'Acadie,* or Acadia, as their own. The explorer and mapmaker Samuel de Champlain was one of the crew. The group landed at the mouth of the St. Croix River in far eastern Maine. Some men remained there to build a settlement while Champlain set off in a sixteen-ton boat with sails and oars. He was to map the coast of Maine and report back.

A few days later, Champlain sailed by a large island. He noted, "It is very high with notches here and there, so that it appears, when one is at sea, like seven or eight mountains rising close together. The tops of most of them are without trees, because they are nothing but rock."[6] He named the

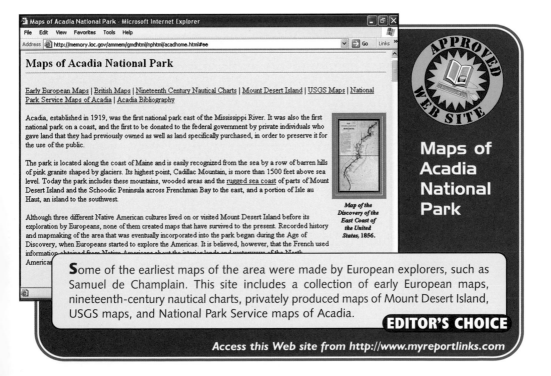

Some of the earliest maps of the area were made by European explorers, such as Samuel de Champlain. This site includes a collection of early European maps, nineteenth-century nautical charts, privately produced maps of Mount Desert Island, USGS maps, and National Park Service maps of Acadia.

EDITOR'S CHOICE

Access this Web site from http://www.myreportlinks.com

island "L'Isle des Monts Deserts," the island of the desert mountains.

THE BATTLE OVER ACADIA

Nine years after Champlain named the island, a group of French Jesuit priests came to the New World. Their plan was to build a mission to serve the Wabanaki. They would call this mission "St. Sauveur," or Holy Savior.

The priests found a sheltered spot and set to work building their new home. It was not to be, however. The British also claimed to own this region of the New World, and their warships patrolled the coast. When the British captain Argall heard about the French mission, he attacked. Some priests escaped in a boat to Nova Scotia. Argall took the rest back to his Virginia headquarters as prisoners.

This skirmish was only the beginning of years of conflict. For hundreds of years, both the French and British claimed to own the coast of Maine. Mount Desert Island was a war front, not a place for peaceful settlers.

Despite this conflict, the French came to the island again. A young explorer named Antoine Laumet gained title to Mount Desert. He pretended to be a French nobleman and changed his name to Antoine de la Mothe, Sieur de Cadillac.[7] He even borrowed a coat of arms from a noble.[8]

Cadillac and his wife came one summer to live on Mount Desert Island. They left after only a few weeks. The next year, in 1689, full scale war broke out between the British and French. Cadillac went on to do great things. He founded the city of Detroit, Michigan, and later became the governor of Louisiana. Although he did not spend much time on Mount Desert Island, its tallest mountain is named for him.

After many years of fighting during the French and Indian Wars, the French lost their territories

A view of Somes Sound, the only fjord on the Atlantic coast of the United States, taken from Acadia Mountain. The sound is nearly five miles long.

in North America. They suffered their final defeat in Quebec. In 1763, the Treaty of Paris gave Acadia to the British, who called it New England and Nova Scotia, not Acadia.

EARLY SETTLERS

In 1761, Mount Desert was a wild, untamed place. Ships regularly sailed by the west coast of the island. Abraham Somes brought his young family to the island that year. Somes felled trees for lumber, and built a small homestead for his wife and daughters near the head of what was later named Somes Sound. The sound is a large fjord that stretches up into the island from the south. A fjord (pronounced fee-ord) looks like a finger of the ocean. Somes Sound is so long that it nearly splits the island in two.

After the American Revolution ended in 1783, more people came to live on the island. The United States and Canada agreed that the St. Croix River would be the border between the two countries. Mount Desert Island was now a part of the new United States.

Eden became the first official town on the island. When it was incorporated in 1796, there were about two hundred residents. In later years, the island folk changed the name of East Eden to Bar Harbor. Today Bar Harbor is by far the largest town on the island. It is a bustling resort full of shops and restaurants.

In the early 1800s, the island was a quiet place. Small villages grew up along the coast. Life revolved around the sea. People fished for herring and cod. Talented carpenters worked in the ship-yards, crafting yachts and schooners. Sailors worked on trade ships, traveling to such far off ports as the West Indies. In those days, ships transported goods from one place to another and carried cargo to ports around the world.

On the interior of the island, people farmed and hunted. Farming was hard work. The soil was rocky, and the growing season was short. People cut down trees to make room for fields, and built mills to saw the lumber into boards and shingles. The mills were powered by water from the rivers. Granite quarries were another source of industry. Men cut the very strong and durable stone from the earth and used it to build churches, libraries, and tombstones.

THOMAS COLE AND THE HUDSON RIVER SCHOOL OF ART

In 1844, Thomas Cole traveled to the island. Cole was a landscape painter. Mount Desert Island was just what he had been looking for. Captivated by the beauty of the land and the sea, he hiked all over the island with his sketch pad. Cole captured some of the island's most spectacular views.

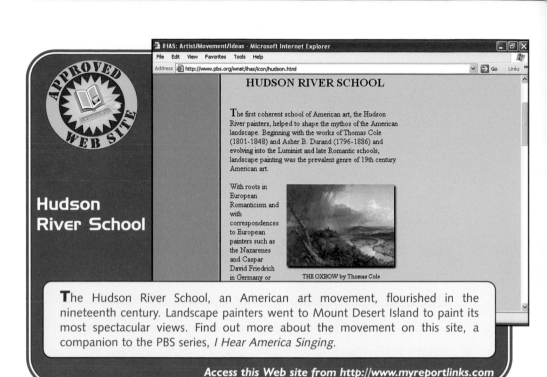

IHAS: Artist/Movement/Ideas - Microsoft Internet Explorer

File   Edit   View   Favorites   Tools   Help

Address http://www.pbs.org/wnet/ihas/icon/hudson.html   Go   Links

HUDSON RIVER SCHOOL

The first coherent school of American art, the Hudson River painters, helped to shape the mythos of the American landscape. Beginning with the works of Thomas Cole (1801-1848) and Asher B. Durand (1796-1886) and evolving into the Luminist and late Romantic schools, landscape painting was the prevalent genre of 19th century American art.

With roots in European Romanticism and with correspondences to European painters such as the Nazarenes and Caspar David Friedrich in Germany or

THE OXBOW by Thomas Cole

Hudson River School

The Hudson River School, an American art movement, flourished in the nineteenth century. Landscape painters went to Mount Desert Island to paint its most spectacular views. Find out more about the movement on this site, a companion to the PBS series, *I Hear America Singing*.

Access this Web site from http://www.myreportlinks.com

At the end of the season, he returned to his home in New York. His paintings sold well. Other artists, such as Frederic Church and Sanford Gifford, followed in Cole's footsteps. They were drawn by the remote beauty of Mount Desert Island. Each of these painters became famous. They were part of a new movement in American art called the Hudson River School. The painters' work celebrated the beauty found in nature.

⊘ RUSTICATORS AND THE SIMPLE LIFE

Unable to forget its magnificence, the artists returned to Mount Desert and brought large parties of their friends with them. They came to rest and relax. There were no hotels at the time, so they rented spare rooms at the homes of farmers or fishermen and their families.

They spent their days outside, trekking around the island. They searched for wildflowers and picnicked on mountaintops. Floating in a rowboat on a lake, they listened to the rattling birdcall of the kingfishers. At dinner, they pulled up chairs around the table with the farmer's or fisherman's family. In the evenings, they played music or conversed in the soft glow of the lamp light.

These folks were the island's first tourists. They made up a name for themselves: the rusticators. They came to the island for a simple, rustic vacation and to enjoy the beauty of nature. When they went back home at the end of their stay, they could not forget the island. They wrote stories about it and painted pictures of it. Other people read their writing and saw their artwork. They, too, began to daydream about visiting Mount Desert one day.

⇨ AN INFLUX OF TOURISTS

In the summer of 1868, getting to Mount Desert suddenly became a great deal easier. A new steamboat service took people from Boston Harbor to Mount Desert Island. Before then, the trip to the island had taken days. First there was a train ride to Portland, Maine. From there, visitors boarded a steamboat as far east as the town of Castine. For the last leg of the trip, they sailed by schooner. Only people with a lot of time to spare could make the trip. But the new steamboat service changed all that. Locals realized there was money to be made. They built inns to cater to the new influx of summer tourists.

Tourists—many from big cities like Boston, New York, and Philadelphia—flocked to the island. Thanks to the modern industrial age, these eastern cities were flush with money. Large factories churned out goods like cotton and wool fabrics. These products generated wealth, but came at a cost. The factories polluted the air and water. The workers lived in crowded conditions without indoor plumbing. In the heat of the summer months, the stench of the cities was unbearable. Those who could afford to escaped for the summer.

➲ WEALTHY "COTTAGERS"

The island became a hot spot for the richest of the rich. In their circles, Bar Harbor was now a "fashionable spa."[9] It attracted such families as the Morgans, Carnegies, Vanderbilts, Pulitzers, Fords, and Rockefellers.

With such wealth at their disposal, these well-to-do families were not content to stay in an inn. They bought land with views looking out over the sea and built their own private summer "cottages." Why they called them cottages is hard to imagine.

A cottage brings to mind a simple dwelling, yet there was nothing simple about the mansions they built. The huge estates had landscaped lawns and gardens, and staffs of butlers, stable boys, maids, and chefs. One street in Bar Harbor was lined with more than sixty of these so-called cottages. People called it Millionaire's Row.

THE RISK OF OVERDEVELOPMENT

As the century drew to an end, the island was more popular than ever before. Charles Eliot grew worried. The president of Harvard College, Eliot spent his summers on Mount Desert Island. He did not want the island to become too crowded or the forests to be cut down to make way for more cottages.

In 1901, Eliot and his friends formed the Hancock County Trustees of Public Reservations in an effort to protect the island. The trustees bought land on the island and nearby coast. The land would be set aside for future generations to enjoy.

FATHER OF ACADIA

George Dorr was one of Eliot's friends. As a child, Dorr spent his summers on Mount Desert Island. When Dorr inherited the family fortune, he went there to live year-round. Dorr had a passion for the island. Like his friend Eliot, he wanted the island to stay the way it was, and so he joined the Hancock County Trustees.

Soon the group owned a large portion of the island. Dorr met with President Woodrow Wilson and asked him to accept the land as a gift for the people of America. President Wilson agreed, and in 1916, Sieur de Monts National Monument was created.

Three years later, Congress declared the land a national park. It was the first national park in the eastern United States. World War I had just come to an end. France and America had helped one another to win the war, and Congress wanted to

The **Woodlawn Museum** in Ellsworth, Maine, is a property of the Hancock County Trustees of Public Reservations, the group responsible for helping to form Acadia National Park. Also known as The Black House, the estate and its grounds were home to three generations of Col. John Black and his family. It is now a public park located near Acadia National Park.

honor the nation's French allies. It named the new park Lafayette National Park. Marquis de Lafayette was a French general who helped the Americans win the Revolutionary War against the British.

Ten years later, a British family made a generous offer. They would give two thousand acres on Schoodic Point to the park, but there was one condition. The name of the park had to be changed to something less French. The family agreed to the name "Acadia National Park." Dorr took the job of park superintendent. Before he died, Dorr had no money left to his name. He had spent his entire fortune on the park that he loved.

Chapter 3

One of the carriage roads built by John D. Rockefeller, Jr., winds its way invitingly through the forest.

Mount Desert Island Becomes a Park

John D. Rockefeller, Jr., gave approximately ten thousand acres of land to Acadia,[1] roughly one third of the park's lands on Mount Desert Island. His help did not end there. He had a vision for how the park should look. He constructed many miles of roads and built gatehouses that looked as if they escaped from the pages of a fairy tale. He shaped what the park looks like today.

Rockefeller was able to do all of this because he was one of the wealthiest men of his day. He was the sole heir to the Standard Oil Company fortune. Rockefeller worked in an office in New York City. But he did not like to be inside, sitting at a desk. He preferred to be outdoors.

Rockefeller and his wife bought a summer cottage on Mount Desert Island in 1910. They enjoyed the peace and quiet of the island. Unlike the city, there was no traffic. There were no loud cars spewing fumes. In fact, a law banned cars from the island. The Rockefellers did not mind. They liked using their horses and carriages. However, the people who lived year-round on the

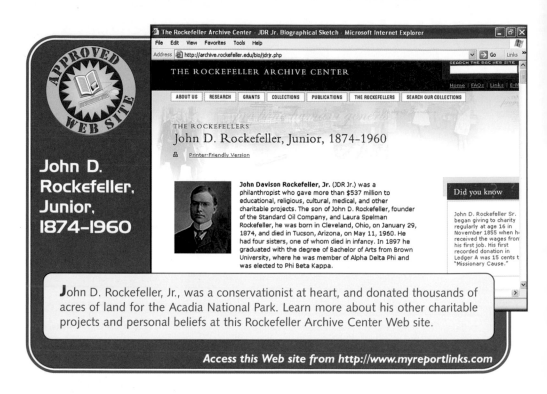

The Rockefeller Archive Center - JDR Jr. Biographical Sketch - Microsoft Internet Explorer

File   Edit   View   Favorites   Tools   Help

Address http://archive.rockefeller.edu/bio/jdrjr.php

THE ROCKEFELLER ARCHIVE CENTER

ABOUT US   RESEARCH   GRANTS   COLLECTIONS   PUBLICATIONS   THE ROCKEFELLERS   SEARCH OUR COLLECTIONS

THE ROCKEFELLERS
John D. Rockefeller, Junior, 1874–1960

Printer-Friendly Version

John Davison Rockefeller, Jr. (JDR Jr.) was a philanthropist who gave more than $537 million to educational, religious, cultural, medical, and other charitable projects. The son of John D. Rockefeller, founder of the Standard Oil Company, and Laura Spelman Rockefeller, he was born in Cleveland, Ohio, on January 29, 1874, and died in Tucson, Arizona, on May 11, 1960. He had four sisters, one of whom died in infancy. In 1897 he graduated with the degree of Bachelor of Arts from Brown University, where he was member of Alpha Delta Phi and was elected to Phi Beta Kappa.

Did you know

John D. Rockefeller Sr. began giving to charity regularly at age 16 in November 1855 when he received the wages from his first job. His first recorded donation in Ledger A was 15 cents to "Missionary Cause."

John D.
Rockefeller,
Junior,
1874–1960

John D. Rockefeller, Jr., was a conservationist at heart, and donated thousands of acres of land for the Acadia National Park. Learn more about his other charitable projects and personal beliefs at this Rockefeller Archive Center Web site.

Access this Web site from http://www.myreportlinks.com

island grew to dislike the ban. They wanted to own cars like other Americans. In 1915, people voted to lift the ban and allow cars.

➔ ROCKEFELLER'S ROADS

People loved riding around the island. It was a tradition among summer folk. The horses didn't go too fast, and there was plenty of time to enjoy the views. A buckboard wagon was just right for bumping along the country roads. The wagons were locally made right there on the island. The buckboard was pulled by a team of horses. Sightseers sat on benches nailed to a simple wooden frame.[2]

Rockefeller did not want to lose this tradition. He didn't want the peace and quiet destroyed by cars. In response to the lifted ban, he built gravel roads on his property. These roads were just for carriage rides—no cars were allowed. When he had built all the roads he could, he asked if he could extend his roads into the park. The park accepted.[3] Between 1915 and 1940, Rockefeller built fifty-seven miles of carriage roads.

The roads still wind through the forest, passing by lakes and ponds. Seventeen stone bridges grace the roads. These charming bridges, made of local stone, are works of art. Some are made of hand-hewn granite, while others are built from beach cobblestones. Forty-five miles of carriage roads now belong to the park. Even today, there are no cars allowed on these groomed, gravel roads.

A portrait of John D. Rockefeller, Jr., taken in approximately 1915.

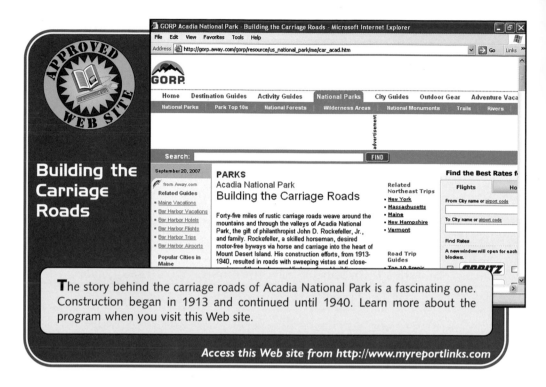

GORP Acadia National Park - Building the Carriage Roads - Microsoft Internet Explorer

File   Edit   View   Favorites   Tools   Help

Address http://gorp.away.com/gorp/resource/us_national_park/me/car_acad.htm   Go   Links »

GORP

Home   Destination Guides   Activity Guides   National Parks   City Guides   Outdoor Gear   Adventure Vaca

National Parks | Park Top 10s | National Forests | Wilderness Areas | National Monuments | Trails | Rivers

Search: [   ] FIND

Building the Carriage Roads

September 20, 2007

from Away.com

Related Guides
- Maine Vacations
- Bar Harbor Vacations
- Bar Harbor Hotels
- Bar Harbor Flights
- Bar Harbor Trips
- Bar Harbor Airports

Popular Cities in Maine

PARKS

Acadia National Park

Building the Carriage Roads

Forty-five miles of rustic carriage roads weave around the mountains and through the valleys of Acadia National Park, the gift of philanthropist John D. Rockefeller, Jr., and family. Rockefeller, a skilled horseman, desired motor-free byways via horse and carriage into the heart of Mount Desert Island. His construction efforts, from 1913-1940, resulted in roads with sweeping vistas and close-

Related Northeast Trips
- New York
- Massachusetts
- Maine
- New Hampshire
- Vermont

Road Trip Guides
- Top 10 Scenic

Find the Best Rates f

Flights   Ho

From City name or airport code
[   ]

To City name or airport code
[   ]

Find Rates

A new window will open for each blocker.

ORBITZ

The story behind the carriage roads of Acadia National Park is a fascinating one. Construction began in 1913 and continued until 1940. Learn more about the program when you visit this Web site.

Access this Web site from http://www.myreportlinks.com

However, people may walk or bicycle on them. The roads are also open to horseback riders. In the winter, cross-country skiers and people on snowshoes use them. At the park's Wildwood Stables, you can even ride in a horse-drawn carriage, just like in Rockefeller's day. The carriage roads are one of the features that make Acadia so special.

Rockefeller recognized that cars would need roads to drive on, too. The Park Service built the Park Loop Road with financial and technical support from Rockefeller. The road is a twenty-seven-mile loop around the east side of the island.

The Park Loop Road features plenty of scenic overlooks. It winds along the shore, by Sand

Beach, Thunder Hole, and Otter Cliffs. Then the road snakes inland to Jordan Pond and Eagle Lake. Famed landscape architect Frederick Law Olmsted, Jr. designed the road to make sure that it passed by the park's best features. It took many years to complete. Today, most visitors to Acadia drive on the Park Loop Road.

➡ THE DECLINE OF THE COTTAGE ERA

Mount Desert Island was a playground for the wealthy during the early 1900s. But that time was drawing to an end. A series of events was soon to

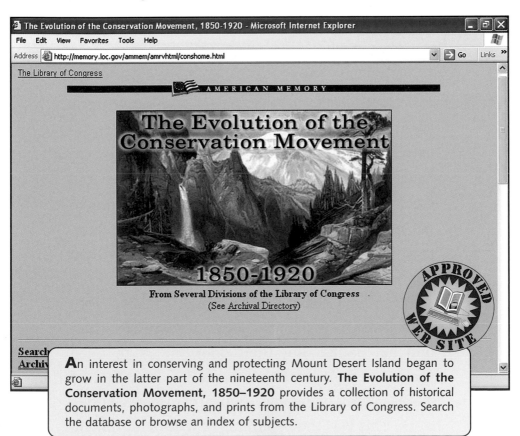

An interest in conserving and protecting Mount Desert Island began to grow in the latter part of the nineteenth century. **The Evolution of the Conservation Movement, 1850–1920** provides a collection of historical documents, photographs, and prints from the Library of Congress. Search the database or browse an index of subjects.

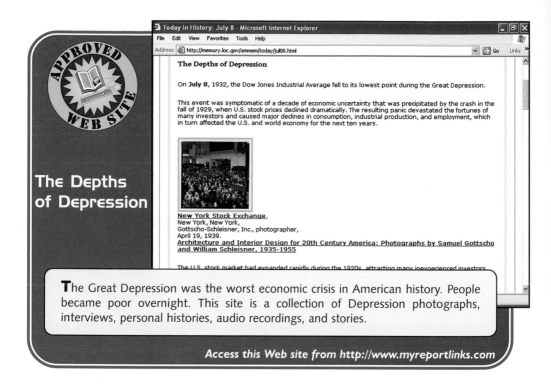

The Depths
of Depression

The Depths of Depression

On **July 8**, 1932, the Dow Jones Industrial Average fell to its lowest point during the Great Depression.

This event was symptomatic of a decade of economic uncertainty that was precipitated by the crash in the fall of 1929, when U.S. stock prices declined dramatically. The resulting panic devastated the fortunes of many investors and caused major declines in consumption, industrial production, and employment, which in turn affected the U.S. and world economy for the next ten years.

New York Stock Exchange,
New York, New York,
Gottscho-Schleisner, Inc., photographer,
April 19, 1939.
Architecture and Interior Design for 20th Century America: Photographs by Samuel Gottscho and William Schleisner, 1935-1955

The U.S. stock market had expanded rapidly during the 1920s, attracting many inexperienced investors.

The Great Depression was the worst economic crisis in American history. People became poor overnight. This site is a collection of Depression photographs, interviews, personal histories, audio recordings, and stories.

Access this Web site from http://www.myreportlinks.com

change life on the island. The first problem was a new income tax of 1913. Each year people would have to report the money they had earned and would have to pay a percentage of that money to the federal government. While the wealthy summer folk still had plenty of money, they now had less to spend on the luxuries of life.

Then, in 1929, the stock market crashed. People's investments and savings disappeared into thin air. Banks shut their doors never to open again. Unemployment increased dramatically, and more and more people found themselves out of work. This was the beginning of a difficult time in

America called the Great Depression, which was to last for ten years.

As if that was not enough, the threat of war hung in the air. Trouble was brewing abroad. Adolf Hitler, the German dictator, had plans to take over Europe. After leading an invasion of Poland, he went on to take over Denmark, Norway, Holland, Belgium, and France. Asia was also in turmoil, as Japan was battling with China. The whole world seemed to be at war. The United States did not want to take part in the war. There were enough problems at home.

Then came the fateful day of December 7, 1941. Enemy planes zoomed low over Hawaii, and

The Herbert Hoover Presidential Library and Museum provides an overview of the Great Depression, including its causes and aftermath. President Hoover's early response to the crisis is also covered.

Access this Web site from http://www.myreportlinks.com

their pilots dropped bombs on Pearl Harbor. Japan had attacked the United States. Americans were in a state of shock. Now there was no choice but for the country to enter World War II. The war cost a great deal of money, and it came at a time when the nation had little money to spare. Americans at home did their part for the war effort. The government established rations on food and gasoline, two goods needed for soldiers on the war front. Now there was no gas to fuel long car trips. Tourist travel ground to a halt. The shops of Bar Harbor stood quiet.

→A BLOWTORCH OF FLAME SHOOTS OVER THE OCEAN

The summer and fall of 1947 were very dry along the New England coast. It had not rained much at all since May on Mount Desert Island. The forests were brittle and withered when a fire started at a town dump on the island.

At first, the fire just smoldered. Firefighters did their best to put it out, but within a short time the weather changed. A strong wind blew across the island from the northwest. The air soon filled with smoke and hot sparks. Fierce gusts of wind drove a wall of fire through the dry forest. One man remembered seeing a tree burst into flame as if it had been doused with gasoline.[4]

The fire burned for ten days, sweeping down the east side of the island. It roared straight down

Millionaire's Row in Bar Harbor. More than sixty cottages were razed to the ground. People were evacuated from the island while firefighters battled the blaze. By the time the fire died out, it had destroyed seventeen thousand acres of land.

While more than a third of the park was burned in all, the western side of the island was unscathed by the inferno. Today, there are still many private mansions standing there. Locals call it the "quiet side" of the island. Bar Harbor became less of a resort for the wealthy. With its shops and restaurants, it attracts tourists of all kinds. Some of the grand cottages have been converted to inns where visitors may stay.

RECOVERY FROM THE FIRE

After the fire, much of the park was a sorry sight. Blackened trees lay on the ground. People feared the forest was ruined. They thought the trees would take a long time to grow back.[5] That was not the case.

The dark evergreen forest was gone, but it made way for a new kind of forest. The fire put many nutrients back into the soil. Now the soil was incredibly rich and fertile. In the past, the dark forest canopy had kept sunlight from reaching the forest floor. Some tree seeds that needed a lot of sunlight to grow never stood a chance in the old forest. Now it was their turn to thrive.

A view of Eagle Lake in autumn.

Maples, birches, oaks, and poplars sprouted the next spring and grew quickly. Visiting the park today, you would never guess there had been a fire at all. However, if you look closely, you can still tell where the fire was. The leaves of the maples, oaks, birches, and poplars change color each autumn. Where the fire did not touch, the forest is mostly spruce, fir, and pine. These trees have needles that stay green, even in winter.

A Tour of the Park

Gone are the days when people came to Acadia by steamship. Today, most people drive to Mount Desert Island. Of course, some people still come to the island by way of the sea. Huge cruise ships dock in Bar Harbor. Thousands of people come ashore to stretch their legs and shop in the boutiques.

The main reason most people drive to the island is to enjoy Acadia National Park. After a stop at the Visitor Center, they travel on the Park Loop Road. The road climbs into the hills, and there are spectacular views off to the east. Down below, one can see the town of Bar Harbor. It sits on the edge of Frenchman Bay. Little rounded islands rise up out of the water. These are the Porcupine Islands, and it is easy to see how they got their name. They really do look like porcupines. Their bristles are the spiky tops of the evergreen trees, their faces the rocky cliffs.

On the other side of the bay, one can see Schoodic Point on the mainland. It forms the tip of

A glimpse of private mansions can be viewed from the Park Loop Road overlooking Frenchman Bay at Acadia National Park. Vacation homes now dot the shores around the park.

Morning sea fog engulfs Bald Porcupine Island, off the coast of Bar Harbor, Maine.

a peninsula of land that juts out into the ocean. Two thousand acres of land on Schoodic Peninsula belong to the park. The Park Loop Road continues on along the shore. It passes the park's most famous attractions: Sand Beach, Thunder Hole, and Otter Cliffs. Then it turns inland, toward Jordan Pond, Cadillac Mountain, and Eagle Lake.

SIEUR DE MONTS SPRING

From the Park Loop Road, there is an exit to Sieur de Monts Spring. The spring is a source of clear, fresh water that bubbles up from underground. An

The **Acadia** Web site offers a comprehensive series of short articles about the park's various features, including Sieur de Monts Spring. It includes information about many of its other attractions as well as a number of maps and photos.

old Wabanaki trail leads to the spring on its way to the coast.[6] The Father of Acadia, George Dorr, bought the spring for the park and had a white well house built over it. The house has pillars and a rounded roof, and there is a plaque here dedicated to Dorr.

The Acadia Nature Center is nearby. Its exhibits tell the story of the natural history of the park. The Wild Gardens of Acadia are next to the spring, too. A pleasant stroll though the gardens teaches about native plants. At the small Abbe Museum at Sieur de Monts Spring, there is a display of ancient artifacts. They were left behind by the first people to live in Maine. The museum also opened a second location in downtown Bar Harbor in 2001. Its space there is much larger and celebrates both the past and present culture of the Wabanaki people.

A QUIETER ACADIA: SCHOODIC PENINSULA

A visit to Schoodic Peninsula is well worth the trouble. A short ferry ride from Bar Harbor carries people the five miles across the bay to this cape. It takes a lot longer to get there by car or bus. It is a fifty-mile drive back onto the mainland and down the other side of Frenchman Bay. The views on the way are breathtaking. The road to Schoodic Point often follows along the water's edge. From here, one can look across the bay to

Waves crashing into the rocks at Schoodic Point, the highlight of Schoodic Peninsula at Acadia National Park.

see the noble mountains of Mount Desert. The road takes a sharp turn in the small fishing village of Winter Harbor. It is here that the ferry from Bar Harbor docks.

Soon after the village, a large sign welcomes people to Acadia's Schoodic Peninsula. If one peers into the dense forest at the edge of the road, it looks as dark as night. The spruce trees grow right up next to one another, their branches tangled together. There is no camping in this part of the park, and there are no crowds of tourists, either. There is a scenic picnic area and several hiking trails. It is very peaceful and remote.

Other than the road, the coast is completely undeveloped. It is easy to imagine it looks much as it did when Champlain sailed by, four hundred years ago. The highlight of Schoodic Peninsula is Schoodic Point. With no islands to break their force, the waves come crashing in from the Atlantic.

ISLE AU HAUT AND THE OTHER ISLANDS OF ACADIA

Isle au Haut is the most remote part of Acadia National Park. This small island lies fifteen miles to the southwest of Mount Desert. Half of the island belongs to the park. About seventy people live on the island year-round. They make their livelihood from fishing.[7] The island boasts ocean views and rocky cliffs.

A mail boat travels to Isle au Haut daily. It leaves from the town of Stonington, Maine, a two-hour car trip from Mount Desert Island. The mail boat carries people and bicycles to the island, but it does not take cars. The park has a campground with lean-to shelters at Duck Harbor. Campers must make reservations ahead of time. Have you ever wanted to know what it's like to sleep in a lighthouse? On Isle au Haut, you can stay at a privately owned lighthouse that has been converted into an inn.

Acadia owns land on eleven other small islands as well. In the summer, park rangers take people by boat to Baker Island. Baker Island lies on the southeast side of Mount Desert. No one lives here anymore, but you can still see the remains of an old homestead. The rangers tell the story of the family who made the island their home.

The Gilley family came to the island in the early 1800s. They farmed the land and fished the seas. When a lighthouse was built on the island in 1828, William Gilley took the job of manning it. The lighthouse beacon still shines today, but there is no longer a lighthouse keeper. Instead, the light runs on solar power.[8]

Chapter 4

Calls of the common loon often echo through Acadia National Park. The loon's black head, black collar band, and red eyes help make it an easy waterbird to identify.

Plants and Animals of Acadia

In Acadia, the winters are cold and dark, and so trees here must make the most of the winter sunlight. Evergreen trees do that best. Evergreen trees grow thin green needles that they keep all year-round. While other trees are busy growing new leaves each spring, evergreen trees still have their needles. They can begin converting sunshine into food right away. Thanks to their pointy shape, these trees can handle heavy snow. The snow slides down the branches to plop on the ground.

Acadia has a boreal forest, or a typical northern forest. It is made up of spruce and fir trees. Spruce trees have short, pointy needles. Red spruce trees *(Picea rubens)* grow on the cliffs near the sea. White spruces grow inland. People call white spruce *(Picea glauca)* by the name skunk spruce because its needles give off a musty smell. Balsam fir trees *(Abies balsamea)* give off a wonderful scent. Fir needles are flat, not sharp like spruce.

Other evergreens grow in the park, too. Eastern white pine *(Pinus strobus)* is the Maine state tree. White pines grow

Acadia National Park - Plants and Wildlife - US-Parks.com - Microsoft Internet Explorer

File   Edit   View   Favorites   Tools   Help

Address http://www.us-parks.com/acadia/plants_and_wildlife.html   Go   Links »

US National Parks & Monuments Travel Guide
US-Parks.com
Go your own way - with our help

Rocky Mountain

Park Locator | Pre Planned Routes | National Parks Lodging | National Parks | Outdoor Gear

Acadia National Park - Plants and Wildlife
Home > Acadia > Park Info > Plants and Wildlife

Animals
Plants
Amphibians, Reptiles and
Mammals
Hawkwatch
Peregrine Falcons
Common Native Plants
Lakes and Forests
Peregrine Falcon Update

:: Lodging
:: Maps
:: Park Info
 · Plants and Wildlife
 - Animals
 - Plants
 - Reptiles
 - Hawkwatch
 - Peregrine Falcons
 - Native Plants
 - Lakes and Forests
 - Falcon Update
 - Ferns
 - Grasses
 - Mosses
 - Wildflowers
 - Wildlife Program
 - Mammals
 · Geology
 · For Kids
 · History
 · Fire Management

Learn more about the park's animals, plants, and geology on **U.S. National Parks & Monuments Travel Guide: Acadia National Park.** Features include details about the park's history, and photographs found throughout the Web site.

EDITOR'S CHOICE

very tall and straight; people used to highly prize their logs for ship masts. The jack pines *(Pinus banksiana)* are short and stubby. Red pines *(Pinus resinosa)* grow tall, with reddish bark. Pitch pines *(Pinus rigida)* thrive in poor, sandy soil.

➲ A COLORFUL AUTUMN DISPLAY

Trees that lose their leaves in the fall are deciduous trees. They live at the edges of the forest, near the sides of the road, and in old fields. Many deciduous trees grew up in the wake of the fire of 1947. The sugar maple tree *(Acer saccharum)* can turn red or gold in the fall. The Wabanaki were the first to collect the tree's sweet sap. When the sap is boiled down, it becomes maple syrup.

Paper birch trees *(Betula papyrifera)* have lovely white bark that peels off in long papery strips. The Wabanaki used the bark to make baskets. The leaves of red oak trees *(Quercus rubra)* have a rich copper color in the fall. The oaks are the last trees to lose their leaves each year. Quaking aspen, or trembling aspen *(Populus tremuloidies),* have small, heart-shaped leaves. When the wind blows, the leaves of the aspen flutter, showing their pale green undersides.

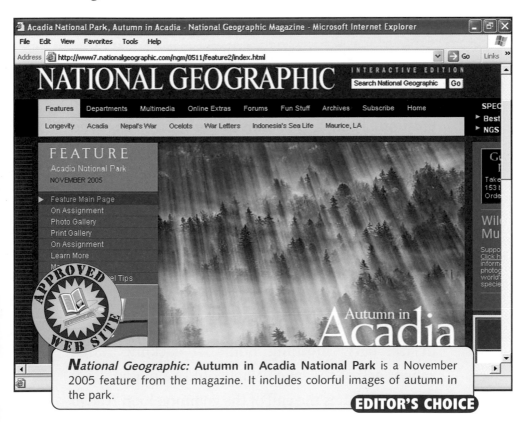

National Geographic: Autumn in Acadia National Park is a November 2005 feature from the magazine. It includes colorful images of autumn in the park.

⊜Life in the Bogs and Swamps

Northern white cedar trees *(Thuja occidentalis)* like to grow in the swamp where it is wet. They have stringy brown bark and their needles are branched. While they may never grow to be very tall, cedars can live to be hundreds of years old. The scraggly black spruce *(Picea mariana)* tree grows in bogs and it has short, bluish-green needles. The American larch tree *(Larix laricina)* makes its home in swamps. Although it has needles, it is not an evergreen. In the fall, all of the needles turn bright gold and drop to the ground. Folks in Maine have their own name for the larch: the hackmatack.

Red maples *(Acer rubrum)* grow so well in swamps that their nickname is the swamp maple. They are the first trees to turn color in the autumn. Their leaves turn a bright crimson. Wild cranberries also grow in Acadia's bogs. The red berries are ripe in the fall. Pitcher plants and sundews are carnivorous bog plants. *Carnivorous* means "meat-eating." These plants attract and trap insects. When the insects' bodies decay, the plants absorb the nutrients.

⊜Two Odd Waterbirds

In the early morning hours, a cackling laugh echoes across the lake. What could be making that eerie noise? It is the call of the common loon *(Gavia immer)*. The loon is a large, ducklike bird that sits low in the water. People in canoes sometimes come upon this shy bird, although it is quick to dive under water. Because a loon can hold its breath for a long time, it is able to resurface far away from where it dives.

With its black head, black collar band, and red eyes, the loon is easy to identify. It makes its home on freshwater lakes in the spring and summer. The birds need quiet spaces to raise their young. They spend the winter in the ocean, near the shores of the island.

The National Park Service's **Acadia National Park Nature Guide** offers an interesting way to learn more about wildlife found in the park. Features of the site include detailed information, photographs, and audio files of bird calls.

Four peregrine chicks at the Precipice huddle together after being banded by the park wildlife biologist.

The Atlantic Puffin *(Fratercula arctica)* lives in the cold ocean near Mount Desert Island. It spends most of its life in the water. When it is time to lay eggs and raise its young, it goes ashore on tiny remote islands. The puffin has a large, triangular beak. It uses its beak to catch the little fish that make up its diet. Its beak is very colorful, with stripes of red, orange, yellow, and gray. Its back and wings

▽ The Atlantic Puffin makes its home in the ocean near Mount Desert Island.

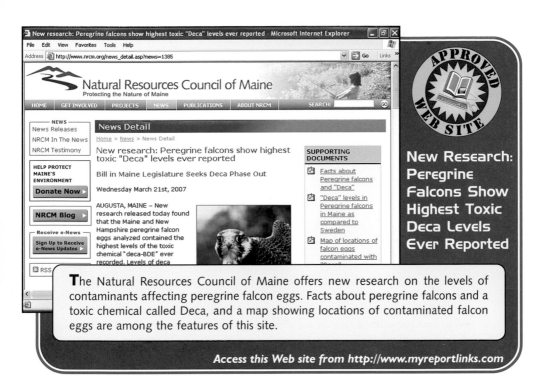

New research: Peregrine falcons show highest toxic "Deca" levels ever reported - Microsoft Internet Explorer

File   Edit   View   Favorites   Tools   Help

Address http://www.nrcm.org/news_detail.asp?news=1385   Go   Links

Natural Resources Council of Maine
Protecting the Nature of Maine

HOME   GET INVOLVED   PROJECTS   NEWS   PUBLICATIONS   ABOUT NRCM   SEARCH: ___ GO

NEWS
News Releases
NRCM In The News
NRCM Testimony

HELP PROTECT MAINE'S ENVIRONMENT
Donate Now ▶

NRCM Blog ▶

Receive e-News
Sign Up to Receive
e-News Updates ▶

RSS

News Detail

Home > News > News Detail

New research: Peregrine falcons show highest toxic "Deca" levels ever reported

Bill in Maine Legislature Seeks Deca Phase Out

Wednesday March 21st, 2007

AUGUSTA, MAINE – New research released today found that the Maine and New Hampshire peregrine falcon eggs analyzed contained the highest levels of the toxic chemical "deca-BDE" ever recorded. Levels of deca

SUPPORTING DOCUMENTS

Facts about Peregrine falcons and "Deca"

"Deca" levels in Peregrine falcons in Maine as compared to Sweden

Map of locations of falcon eggs contaminated with "Deca"

New Research: Peregrine Falcons Show Highest Toxic Deca Levels Ever Reported

The Natural Resources Council of Maine offers new research on the levels of contaminants affecting peregrine falcon eggs. Facts about peregrine falcons and a toxic chemical called Deca, and a map showing locations of contaminated falcon eggs are among the features of this site.

Access this Web site from http://www.myreportlinks.com

are black, while the feathers on its belly are white. A puffin's call sounds like a chain saw, "Rrrrr, Rrrrr."

⊝ DDT AND THE PEREGRINE FALCON

What kind of bird can dive through the air at speeds of over one hundred miles per hour? The peregrine falcon *(Falco peregrinus)* can. A bird that hunts other birds, it dives full force at its unsuspecting prey and grabs it with its sharp talons. The bird has a small head, a speckled white breast, gray feathers on its back, and yellow legs. When it flies, it displays its long, narrow tail and pointed wings. Peregrines nest on rocky ledges on cliffs that overlook the sea.

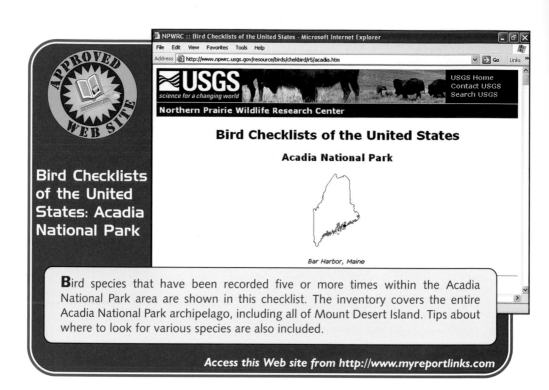

USGS Home
Contact USGS
Search USGS

≈USGS
science for a changing world

Northern Prairie Wildlife Research Center

Bird Checklists of the United States

Acadia National Park

Bar Harbor, Maine

Bird Checklists of the United States: Acadia National Park

Bird species that have been recorded five or more times within the Acadia National Park area are shown in this checklist. The inventory covers the entire Acadia National Park archipelago, including all of Mount Desert Island. Tips about where to look for various species are also included.

Access this Web site from http://www.myreportlinks.com

Sadly, by the mid-1900s there were no peregrines left in Acadia. A chemical called DDT was to blame. People used DDT to kill insects that carried disease. But it did more than poison the insects; it also poisoned small birds that ate the insects. The birds did not die from the poison, but they did store the toxins in their bodies.

Peregrines are at the top of the food chain. They eat small birds, and many of these were toxic with DDT. The poison made the peregrines' eggshells too thin. Their eggs broke, and no new chicks were born. Too late, people realized what had happened. They outlawed DDT in the United States in the 1970s.

➡️ PEREGRINE CHICK EXPERIMENT

In 1984, Acadia became the site of an experiment. Biologists took eggs from peregrine falcons that were bred in captivity. They watched over the eggs as they hatched. Then they took the chicks to a nest site on a cliff and left them there to grow. They sent food to them through a long tube. As the falcons grew up, they learned to hunt their own food. The biologists watched over the chicks from afar.[1]

Their hard work was rewarded. In 1987, the first peregrine returned to the park. In 1991, he and his mate hatched their first chicks. In 2006, there were four pairs of nesting falcons in Acadia.[2] The park closes down hiking trails near the nest sites at certain times of the year. They want to make the birds feel welcome, especially when they have young chicks. This is also done for safety reasons: the parents will dive at people to protect their chicks. Peregrines are still on the state's list of endangered species.

Bald eagles *(Haliaeetus leucocephalus)* soar over the water, looking for fish. With wingspans of eight feet, they are quite an impressive sight. Eagle pairs build a huge nest of sticks, up high in a tall tree. An adult eagle has a white tail, brown body, white head, and a bright yellow beak. Eagles are also on the endangered species list in Maine. Like the peregrines, the eagles were poisoned by

DDT. Fortunately, these grand birds are making a comeback. One hundred and fifty pairs now live in Maine.

BIRDS ON THE SHORE AND SEA

With a pair of binoculars and a good guidebook to birds, a visitor to the park can see many water-birds as they bob in the ocean waves. Seagulls glide above the shore and look for food. Two kinds of seagulls are common in Acadia: the her-ring gull *(Larus argentatus)* and the greater black-backed gull *(Larus marinus)*. Gulls are scav-engers. They feed on trash that people leave behind. Some visitors bring bread and feed them on purpose, but this is not a good idea. Because of humans and their trash, the gulls' numbers are increasing. They became a threat to other seabirds.

The double-crested cormorant *(Phalacrocorax auritus)* is a large waterbird. It likes to find a rock to stand on and then spreads its wings wide. The bufflehead *(Bucephala islandica)* is a small white duck with black feathers on its back and face. It has puffy white feathers on the top of its head that make it look as if it is wearing a white bonnet.

The red-breasted merganser *(Mergus serrator)* is easy to spot. Its feathers stick up in a spiky Mohawk on the back and top of its head. Black guillemots *(Cepphus grylle)* are noisy, squawking birds with bright red feet. The common eider *(Somateria mollissima)* is a large duck that eats shellfish. It even eats the shells!

Large flocks of white Arctic terns *(Sterna paradisaea)* come here to nest each spring. In the winter, they fly thousands of miles to the icy waters of Antarctica.[3] The surf scoter is a black duck with white spots on its head. Because of its coloring, people sometimes call it the skunk duck.

➔ MAMMALS OF THE ACADIAN FOREST

Many of the animals that live in Acadia are shy. When they hear or smell a person, they are quick to hide. The best way to see the wildlife is to find an out-of-the-way spot. Sit there quietly and wait. With some luck, you will see an animal going about its day.

There are many white-tailed deer *(Odocoileus virginianus)* on the island. They are tawny-colored animals with white bellies and hoofed feet. The babies, called fawns, are born with white spots on their backs. The spots help them to blend in with the forest floor. This is important, as the mother deer leaves her fawn to sleep while she browses for food.

In the summer, deer can be seen at dusk or dawn, feeding on grass at the edge of a meadow. When they are startled, they raise their tails like a white flag and bound away. Deer are very quiet animals, though the males sometimes snort loudly. In the winter, deer make trails through the snowy bogs and nibble on the tender new growth of trees. During snowstorms, the deer take shelter under evergreen trees.

Yips and yowls echo frequently through the night. These are the sounds of a pack of eastern coyotes *(Canis latrans)*. This doglike animal is smaller than a wolf. Farmers worried about their livestock shot coyotes on sight in the past. Today, coyotes are making a comeback in Acadia. The eastern coyote mostly eats small rodents, like mice, shrews, and voles. It is the only predator on the island that hunts the deer. While a healthy

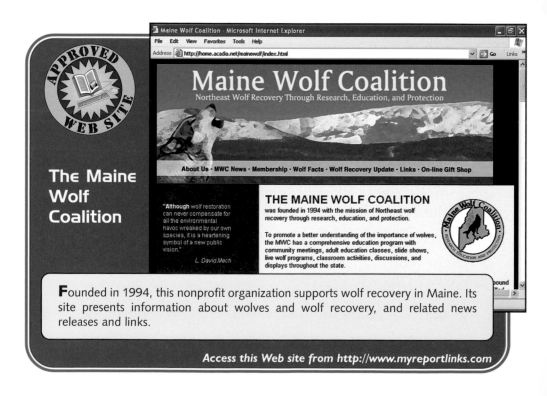

The Maine Wolf Coalition

Founded in 1994, this nonprofit organization supports wolf recovery in Maine. Its site presents information about wolves and wolf recovery, and related news releases and links.

Access this Web site from http://www.myreportlinks.com

▲ *A white-tailed deer shown with its fawn. The white spots on a fawn's back help it to blend in with the forest floor when the mother leaves it to search for food.*

adult deer could outrun a pack of coyotes, the coyotes will chase a weak deer until it is exhausted.

Another source of food for the coyote is the snowshoe hare *(Lepus americanus)*. In the winter, the snowshoe hare's brown fur coat turns bright white. This helps it to blend in with the snow. When it senses danger, the hare freezes. It can stay completely still. If an enemy spots it, the hare will run for its life. Hares can sprint at speeds of up to thirty miles an hour, and jump up to twelve feet in a single hop.[4]

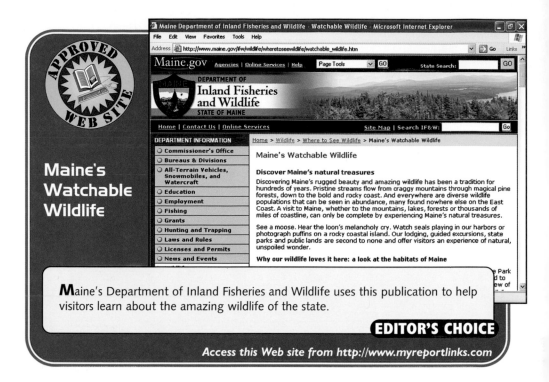

Maine's Watchable Wildlife

Maine's Department of Inland Fisheries and Wildlife uses this publication to help visitors learn about the amazing wildlife of the state.

EDITOR'S CHOICE

Access this Web site from http://www.myreportlinks.com

A red fox slinks through a field, hunting for mice and insects. With its beautiful long rust-colored fur and bushy tail, the fox *(Vulpes fulva)* is easy to spot. Each spring, foxes have a litter of young called kits. Meanwhile, little red squirrels *(Tamiasciurus hudsonicus)* run back and forth on a tree limb, scolding anyone who comes too near.

Black bears *(Urus americanus)* and moose *(Alces alces)* are both quite common in Maine. The black bear can grow up to four hundred fifty pounds. Black bears are shy and usually run away long before you spot them. A mother will attack to protect her young, so never try to approach a bear.

Moose are huge animals, larger than a horse. Perhaps because they are so big, they are often not afraid of people. In the heat of the summer, moose stand in ponds, munching the plants they find on the bottom. In the winter, they eat the buds of trees and shrubs. The males grow large antlers, which they shed each year. Although people occasionally spot bears and moose in Acadia, it is rare.[5]

If you surprise a beaver *(Castor canadensis)*, you will hear a loud slap. The beaver whacks its broad, flat tail on the surface of the pond to warn

▽ *Three young red fox kits venture out of their den.*

its family. Beavers are large rodents who spend most of their time in the water. Like all rodents, they have sharp, strong teeth that never stop growing. They are always wearing their teeth down with the work they do.

Beavers use their teeth to cut down trees. They drag the logs into the water, where they use them to build dams and lodges. A dam blocks the path of a stream. The water builds up behind the dam, creating a pond for the beaver to live in. A lodge is the beaver family's home. It looks like a big mound of sticks in the water. The door to the lodge is underwater. The beaver swims in and then climbs up into its nest. It is fun to watch beavers float on their backs, grasping a branch in their paws while munching away at the leaves.

⊜Mammals of the Sea

Harbor seals *(Phoca vitulina)* bask in the sun on the rocks at low tide. They have no feet and are clumsy out of the water. In the water, their flippers help them dive deep to catch fish to eat. Harbor seals grow to be five feet long. Their eyes are big, dark, and expressive.

Atlantic Harbor porpoises *(Phocoena phocoena)* spend their entire lives in the sea. Unlike fish, sea mammals must come to the surface to get air to breathe. Porpoises are dolphinlike animals that are gray on top and white underneath. These graceful animals like to swim in groups. When they come to the surface, they blow air out from the blowholes on the top of their heads. This makes a loud snorting sound.

Finback whales *(Balaenoptera physalus)* whistle when they come up for air.[6] These gentle creatures are as large as a school bus, and feed on tiny sea animals called plankton. Their mouths are built to strain the plankton from the water. Strips of bone called baleen hang from the roofs of their mouths. When they close their mouths, they can push water through the baleen. The plankton stays in their mouth, ready to eat.

Chapter 5

A view of Little Long Pond in Acadia National Park.

Preserving Acadia for the Future

Acadia is the only national park in New England. In fact, it is the only one in the entire Northeast—a place where many Americans live. That is one of the reasons Acadia is on the top ten list of most-visited national parks.[1] Around 2 million people come to the park each year, and the numbers just keep growing. Americans are exploring their national parks now more than ever before. This is great news for Acadia. The more that people understand and appreciate the park, the better off it will be.

And yet all of these visitors are also bad news for the park. Two million is a great deal of people in a wilderness area. Even if all of those people treat the land with care and respect, they still have a considerable impact. Can that many people enjoy nature and still keep it wild? This concern has caused some people to ask: "Are we loving the park to death?"

People impact the park in many ways. One thing they affect is the air. The air in Acadia is so refreshing. It feels pure

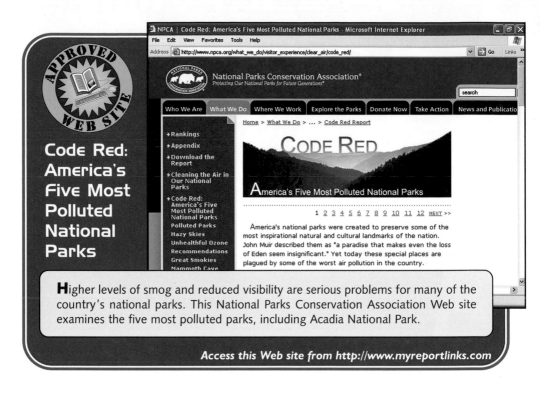

Access this Web site from http://www.myreportlinks.com

Higher levels of smog and reduced visibility are serious problems for many of the country's national parks. This National Parks Conservation Association Web site examines the five most polluted parks, including Acadia National Park.

and clean. But how long will the air stay that way? People come to the island by car, bus, cruise ship, and plane. All of these vehicles burn fuel. When the fuel burns, it creates more than just energy. It also creates by-products, and some of them are toxic. These by-products are not good for the environment.

Pollution comes to the island from far away, too. Acadia is downwind from many big factories and cities. The wind carries the pollutants across the countryside toward the coast of Maine.[2] When it rains, the toxins fall to the ground. When the air is full of pollutants, it looks smoggy. Like fog, smog makes it hazy and hard to see very far.

There is a hazecam on top of McFarland Hill. The camera takes a picture of the view from the northeast across Frenchman Bay. It helps scientists keep an eye on air pollution at Acadia.

➡ ISLAND EXPLORER BUSES

One way that the park is fighting air pollution is with a new bus system. The Island Explorer buses first began to run in 1999. The buses use propane for fuel. Propane burns cleaner than regular gasoline and diesel.[3] Thus the buses are better for the environment. They also help tourists save money on gas. Visitors no longer need a car to explore the park. They can park their cars and

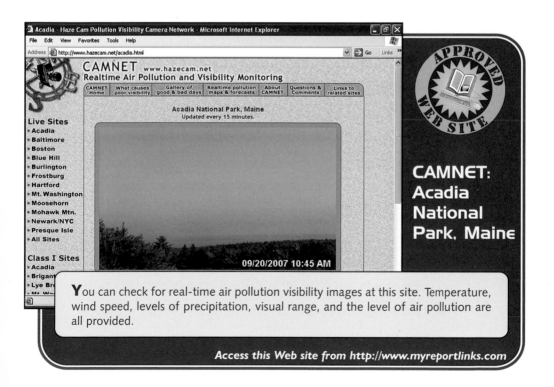

You can check for real-time air pollution visibility images at this site. Temperature, wind speed, levels of precipitation, visual range, and the level of air pollution are all provided.

Access this Web site from http://www.myreportlinks.com

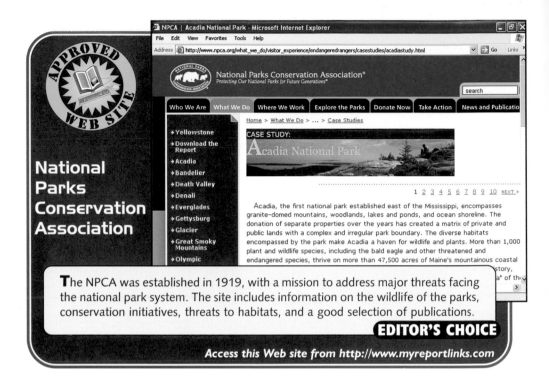

NPCA | Acadia National Park - Microsoft Internet Explorer

File   Edit   View   Favorites   Tools   Help

Address http://www.npca.org/what_we_do/visitor_experience/endangeredrangers/casestudies/acadiastudy.html   Go   Links

National Parks Conservation Association®
Protecting Our National Parks for Future Generations®

search

Who We Are | What We Do | Where We Work | Explore the Parks | Donate Now | Take Action | News and Publicatio

Home > What We Do > ... > Case Studies

→Yellowstone
→Download the Report
→Acadia
→Bandelier
→Death Valley
→Denali
→Everglades
→Gettysburg
→Glacier
→Great Smoky Mountains
→Olympic

CASE STUDY:
Acadia National Park

1 2 3 4 5 6 7 8 9 10 NEXT >

Acadia, the first national park established east of the Mississippi, encompasses granite-domed mountains, woodlands, lakes and ponds, and ocean shoreline. The donation of separate properties over the years has created a matrix of private and public lands with a complex and irregular park boundary. The diverse habitats encompassed by the park make Acadia a haven for wildlife and plants. More than 1,000 plant and wildlife species, including the bald eagle and other threatened and endangered species, thrive on more than 47,500 acres of Maine's mountainous coastal

The NPCA was established in 1919, with a mission to address major threats facing the national park system. The site includes information on the wildlife of the parks, conservation initiatives, threats to habitats, and a good selection of publications.

EDITOR'S CHOICE

Access this Web site from http://www.myreportlinks.com

ride the bus. They do not have to struggle to find a parking spot during peak season.

The bus picks people up in Bar Harbor, shuttles them from the campgrounds and hotels, and makes stops at most of the attractions. At some bus stops, a digital display tells riders when the next bus will come. It is also possible to flag a bus down. Best of all, the buses are free to the public. There is no fare to pay. You can even bring along your dog or your bike.

At this point, the Island Explorer buses run only in the summer. After all, the Park Loop Road closes down in the winter. With the snow and ice, it is not safe. On the other hand, the fall season is a busy time at the park. Thanks to a $1 million donation from L.L. Bean, an outdoor outfitting company based in Freeport, Maine, the buses stayed on the road for the fall foliage season in 2006.

One thing is for sure: the buses help to save Acadia's air. When people take the bus, they do not pollute the air with their car fumes. Since 1999, the buses have kept 33.7 tons of toxins out of the air.[4]

→ FRAGILE MOUNTAIN SUMMITS

It is a lot of fun to hike in Acadia National Park. The views from the mountaintops make the effort well worth it. About three out of every four visitors to the park take some time to enjoy a hike.[5]

As you can imagine, hundreds of thousands of people tramping up a trail can cause damage. The mountain summits are fragile environments. In some ways, the plants and lichens that grow there are tough. They have to be, for they face many challenges. There is little protection from the elements, so they must deal with the whipping wind, the pouring rain, and piles of snow. They have only a very thin layer of soil to take root in.

On top of this, they have to withstand the steps of hikers who stray off the trails. Just one footstep can cause one of these fragile plants considerable harm. Some of these tiny plants take hundreds of

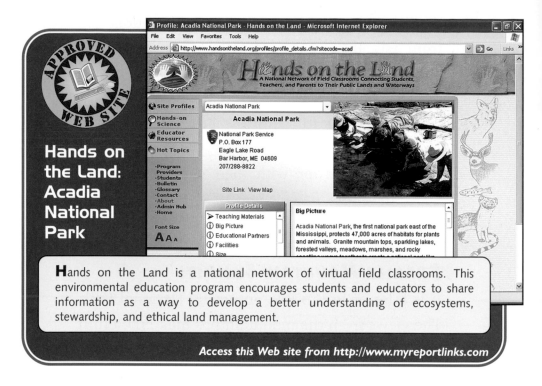

Hands on the Land: Acadia National Park

Hands on the Land is a national network of virtual field classrooms. This environmental education program encourages students and educators to share information as a way to develop a better understanding of ecosystems, stewardship, and ethical land management.

Access this Web site from http://www.myreportlinks.com

years to grow. During the summer, college students take intern jobs as ridge runners in Acadia. Ridge runners hike the trails and keep them in good order. They talk with hikers and teach them about the fragile plants.

To help protect the plants, the park staff works hard at keeping people on the trails. In the forest, they paint blazes on trees to mark the trail. On the barren mountaintops, there are no trees to blaze. There they use loose stones to build cairns to lead the way. *Cairn* is a Scottish word that means "pile of rocks."[6]

Cairns look like fun to build. It takes patience to balance the stones just so. Yet signs in Acadia warn people not to build new cairns along the trails or tamper with the cairns that are there.[7] Cairns are vital tools that serve to mark the trail. Not only do they protect the plants, they guide people in foggy or stormy weather.

→ LEAVE NO TRACE

The National Park Service is a government agency that is in charge of the parks. It must protect the parks along with the plants and animals that live there. The park service must also make each park a place for people to enjoy. It keeps the parks in good condition for future generations, too. It can be a difficult balancing act. The park service needs

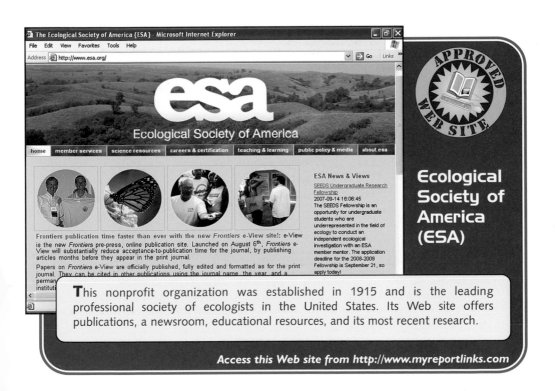

Ecological Society of America (ESA)

This nonprofit organization was established in 1915 and is the leading professional society of ecologists in the United States. Its Web site offers publications, a newsroom, educational resources, and its most recent research.

Access this Web site from http://www.myreportlinks.com

the help of the people who visit the park. That is how the Leave No Trace program began.[8]

Leave No Trace is a program that teaches people how to enjoy nature while protecting it. It educates people to take good care of the land, and it teaches them how to do their part for the future of the park. One principle of the program is: "Take nothing but photos, leave nothing but footprints."

It is tempting to pocket a seashell or a pebble to take home as a memento. But just imagine if every visitor brought a few things home. Millions of pieces of the park would disappear each year! Under the principles of Leave No Trace, people leave the park as they find it. Instead, they can

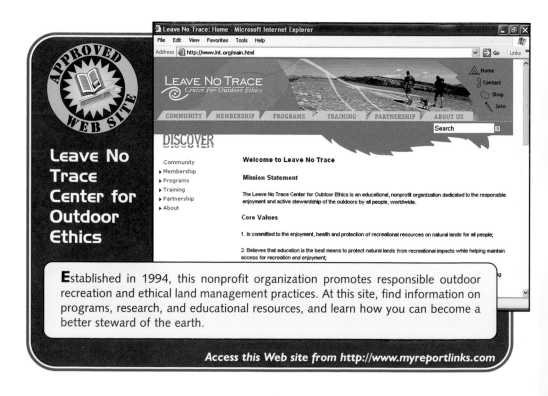

Leave No Trace Center for Outdoor Ethics

Established in 1994, this nonprofit organization promotes responsible outdoor recreation and ethical land management practices. At this site, find information on programs, research, and educational resources, and learn how you can become a better steward of the earth.

Access this Web site from http://www.myreportlinks.com

take photographs during their trip. They can share the photos with people at home. The pictures remind them of their adventures without causing harm to the park.

The park service also asks people not to leave anything behind. They teach people to carry out what they carried in. Did you know that a plastic bag can take ten to twenty years to decompose? A banana peel may last about five weeks. A glass bottle, on the other hand, will not break down for a million years.[9] The park service encourages people to recycle. There are bins where visitors may recycle their glass, aluminum, and plastics. In a recent year, the park recycled twenty-five tons of waste.

Do Not Feed the Animals

Some wild animals will eat whatever they can find. When people leave food out, animals come and eat it. Sometimes people leave food out on purpose, with hopes of luring shy animals out into the open where they can see them. These smart animals learn that where there are people, there is food. In time, they grow bold around people.

In some parts of the country, this happens with bears. Bears, like most wild animals, normally shy away from people. But bears that have learned to eat human food are no longer shy. They can become a very dangerous threat to people. Sadly, the only answer is often to shoot the bear. In Acadia, bears are not a problem. Still, campers may wake up to hear an animal tearing through their trash, looking for food scraps. The culprit is most likely a raccoon or a skunk. The park staff teaches people not to leave food out where animals may find it. They provide animal-proof garbage cans.

INVASION OF THE PLANTS

Can a plant be a villain? It could be argued that purple loosestrife is a bully. Purple loosestrife is a flowering plant that grows where it is wet and marshy. It is not native to America; people brought it here from Europe. They planted it in their gardens to enjoy its lovely violet-colored blooms. The plant soon escaped into the wild, where it has begun to invade the countryside.

Loosestrife thrives in wetlands. It grows so well that it takes over and chokes out the native plants. Since 1988, purple loosestrife has been on the park's hit list. Each year, the staff inspects the wetlands. When they spot purple loosestrife, they treat it with herbicide.[10]

FRIENDS OF ACADIA

The government of the United States owns Acadia National Park. It provides the funds to run the park. Each year, Congress allots money to the park. The funds often fall short. There is not enough money in the budget to take good care of the park. That is where the Friends of Acadia comes in. It is a nonprofit organization devoted to the park. The Friends of Acadia was founded in 1986. It raises money for the park and handles many cleanup projects.

One way the organization helps the park is through the Acadia Trails Forever campaign. Acadia has about one hundred and twenty miles of hiking trails. The trails are old, and some are in rough shape. They need to be fixed. Friends of Acadia raised $9 million to help the cause. The

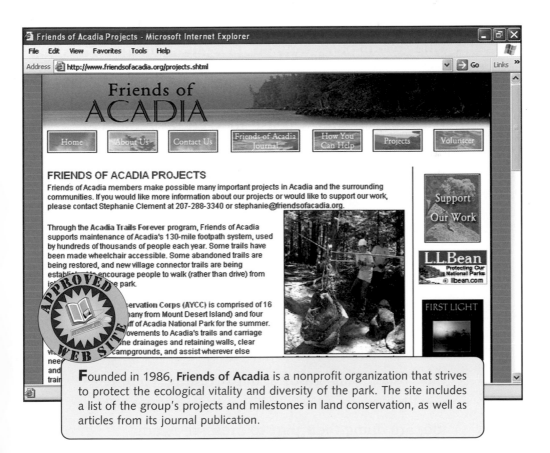

Founded in 1986, **Friends of Acadia** is a nonprofit organization that strives to protect the ecological vitality and diversity of the park. The site includes a list of the group's projects and milestones in land conservation, as well as articles from its journal publication.

park will raise another $5 million, and will spend the money to repair the trails. There will be money left over to keep the trails in good shape for years to come. In a similar way, Friends of Acadia is working with the park to provide the upkeep for the carriage roads.

REDUCING NOISE AND POLLUTION

The Friends of Acadia wants to reduce pollution in and near the park. It worked to establish the Island Explorer bus system,[11] and it is also working to pass laws to keep the park a quiet place. One recent law banned personal watercrafts, which are no longer allowed on Acadia's lakes and ponds. People like personal watercrafts (such as jet skis) because they go fast, but they also pollute the water. If the water is polluted, it is not a good home for fish. These machines also have very noisy motors that scare away the birds and wildlife that live on and near the lakes.

The group would like to take it a step further. It is also pushing to ban personal watercrafts on the saltwater bays and harbors near Acadia. The Friends of Acadia organization is just twenty years old, but it has done great things for the park in that time. This group's hardworking volunteers are like Dorr and Rockefeller before them. They, too, are doing their part to preserve Acadia.

⇒ STEWARDSHIP

Visitors to Acadia quickly see how special a place it is. They are thankful that, one hundred years ago, people had the vision to preserve this land. Acadia National Park can remain the beautiful, wild place that it is today, but not without work. It will need good stewardship from the people of today. With care, Acadia will be there for future generations to enjoy, too.

Chapter

6

The Bass Harbor Head Lighthouse, built in 1858, is now automated and maintained by the Coast Guard.

Things to Do and See in Acadia

The best way to see Acadia National Park is to set off by foot. In a car, the scenery whizzes by. On foot, it is easy to gaze around and see the details. In the late fall, the clusters of bright red winterberries stand out as they cling to the bare branches. In the spring, before all the leaves are out, the delicate white flowers of the shadbush are easy to spot. Smell the fragrant needles of the balsam fir as you walk through the forest. Hear the pounding waves crash and the water gurgle through the stones along the shore. Listen to the songbirds as they call to one another.

There are tough hiking trails for those who like the challenge. The Precipice is probably the toughest climb in the park. This hiking trail goes straight up the cliff face of Champlain Mountain. Hikers must climb hand over hand up iron rungs set into the rock. There are the smooth carriage roads for those who need to go slow. A nice level nature trail runs around Jordan

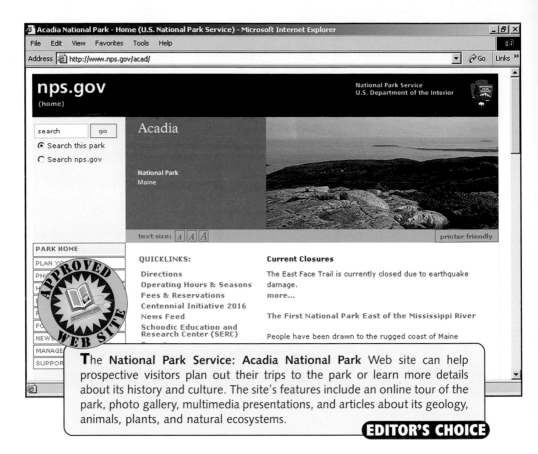

The **National Park Service: Acadia National Park** Web site can help prospective visitors plan out their trips to the park or learn more details about its history and culture. The site's features include an online tour of the park, photo gallery, multimedia presentations, and articles about its geology, animals, plants, and natural ecosystems.

EDITOR'S CHOICE

Pond. The pond is surrounded by picturesque mountains.

Looking for great ocean views? The Ocean Trail is a walking path that follows a portion of the shoreline along the Park Loop Road. Although it is easy to drive to the top of Cadillac Mountain, it is very satisfying to make the climb up the park's tallest peak. People at the parking lot on top will surely be impressed.

Biking around the island is another great way to see Acadia. Bikes are allowed on the carriage trails. The Park Loop Road is accessible to bicycles, too, but watch out for cars. Although the speed limit is slow, drivers may be paying more attention to the scenery than the road. Forgot to bring your bicycle? It is easy to rent one for the day in Bar Harbor. It is against the rules to take a bike on hiking trails in Acadia. At the park's Wildwood Stables, there are horse-drawn carriage rides. They also rent stable space to people who want to bring their own horse.

Perhaps the best way to explore the park is to take a tour led by a park ranger. A ranger will be able to show you a side of Acadia you might never find on your own, and also answer questions you have along the way. Learn about a wide range of subjects, from astronomy to wildlife to the history of the carriage trails. With the help of the park staff, watch those amazing hunters of the sky, the peregrine falcons. Find a specific list of which tours are happening and when they're scheduled in the park newspaper, the *Beaver Log*.

CAMPING UNDER THE STARS

Is there anything better than sitting around the campfire, gazing up at the dark, starry sky? There are two campgrounds on Mount Desert Island that are run by the park. Blackwoods Campground, on the east side of the island, is open year-round. The campsites are in the forest, not far from the shore. In the summer, you must have a reservation to get a tent site in this busy campground.

A lone bicyclist enjoys a ride on one of Acadia National Park's forty-five miles of carriage roads.

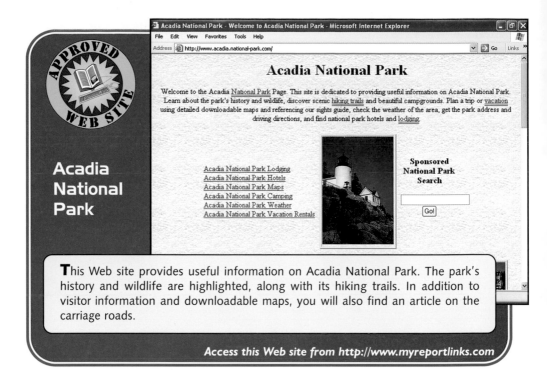

Acadia National Park - Welcome to Acadia National Park - Microsoft Internet Explorer

File   Edit   View   Favorites   Tools   Help

Address | http://www.acadia.national-park.com/ | Go   Links »

Acadia National Park

Welcome to the Acadia National Park Page. This site is dedicated to providing useful information on Acadia National Park. Learn about the park's history and wildlife, discover scenic hiking trails and beautiful campgrounds. Plan a trip or vacation using detailed downloadable maps and referencing our sights guide, check the weather of the area, get the park address and driving directions, and find national park hotels and lodging.

Acadia National Park Lodging
Acadia National Park Hotels
Acadia National Park Maps
Acadia National Park Camping
Acadia National Park Weather
Acadia National Park Vacation Rentals

Sponsored National Park Search

[   ]   Go!

Acadia National Park

This Web site provides useful information on Acadia National Park. The park's history and wildlife are highlighted, along with its hiking trails. In addition to visitor information and downloadable maps, you will also find an article on the carriage roads.

Access this Web site from http://www.myreportlinks.com

Seawall Campground is also on the quiet, east side of the island. It is only open for the summer season, from late May through September.

There are also many private campgrounds on Mount Desert Island, outside of the park. For an even more serene experience, take the ferry to Isle au Haut. At Duck Harbor Campground, on the southeast of the island, the park has several lean-to shelters. Only people with reservations are allowed to spend the night.

⊛ SAMPLING THE LOCAL CUISINE

Lobsters are on the menu on the Maine seacoast and are considered quite a delicacy. The American lobster is a crustacean that lives on the ocean floor. It has two large claws and eight tiny legs. It uses its claws to catch the mussels and clams that it eats. But as the lobster grows, its hard shell no longer fits. Then it molts, or sheds, its shell. While its new shell is growing, the lobster finds a safe place to hide.

Lobsters can grow to be over four feet long and weigh up to forty pounds. But the lobsters found in restaurants weigh only a pound or two. People catch lobsters in baited traps. They let the traps sink to the bottom of the sea, and a colorful buoy marks the trap's location. Lobsters can climb into the traps, but they cannot climb out again. Maine harvests millions of lobsters each year.

⇒ LOBSTER ON THE MENU

In the summer, lobster rolls (a sandwich roll filled with lobster meat mixed with mayonnaise) are a popular lunch. And if you want to have a true Maine experience, try eating boiled lobster. Did you know that a lobster's shell turns red only when it is cooked? Live lobsters have dark green shells. A whole lobster is boiled or steamed in seawater, then plunked straight from the pot onto a plate. It is very messy to eat, and one usually dons a bib for this dining experience.

Then crack open the lobster shell, using your hands and a tool called a lobster cracker. Use a lobster pick, a thin metal hook, to pry the meat out of the shell. The best meat is in the tail and the claws. It tastes sweet and rich, especially after it is dunked in melted butter. People also savor the tiny bits of meat in the legs and flippers at the end of the tail. Inside the body, you may see green toma-lley. That is the liver and pancreas—some people love it, while others would never touch it.

Maine lobsters are a luxury food, and are shipped all over the world today. That was not the case one hundred and fifty years ago. Then they were so common that you could pick them off the beach at low tide. Back then, people made use of lobsters to fertilize crops, not to eat.

➔ SATISFY YOUR SWEET TOOTH

If the idea of lobster does not appeal to you, maybe some ice cream would. At Mount Dessert Island Ice Cream in downtown Bar Harbor, the ice cream is handmade on site. For some local flavor, try the blueberry basil or Maine cranberry sorbet. The ice cream parlor mixes flavors to make some out-of-this-world ice cream. Campers may want to try a cone of the S'mores flavor.

Ben and Bill's Chocolate Emporium is an old-fashioned candy store in Bar Harbor. It is the place to go for saltwater taffy. The store also serves ice cream—even lobster-flavored ice cream! Enjoy your ice-cream cone while taking a stroll by the ocean. Bar Harbor's Shore Path starts by the town pier. It is an easy walk along the paved trail. There are views of Frenchman Bay and the breakwater, which is man-made. The waves crash against it and lose their force before entering the harbor.

⇒ WINTER WONDERLAND

A fresh blanket of bright snow covers the carriage trail in the winter. The woods are quiet and peaceful, and the snow muffles all sounds. The sun shines on the ice that covers the bare branches of the trees. The spruce and fir trees wear white caps of snow. Pull on a warm pair of boots, pack a thermos of hot tea, and hit the trails. Bring a guidebook that explains animal tracks. Winter is a great time to go on an animal safari at Acadia. The animals leave their tracks in the snow. Squirrels leave behind footprints and the cases of the seeds they nibbled on. Wing marks and fur show where an owl pounced on a mouse.

⇒ EXPLORE A TIDE POOL

The ocean tide rises and falls twice a day on the Maine coast. At high tide, the ocean's waves come far up onto shore. At low tide, the waves recede and expose more of the rocky shoreline. Why does the water move back and forth each day? It is the moon that causes the tides to rise and fall. The moon is always circling around the earth. It is held

A shallow tide pool at Acadia National Park. The pools are home to many tiny plants such as seaweed, rockweed, kelp, and Irish moss, and animals such as snails, mussels, and barnacles.

in place by the earth's gravitational pull. As the moon travels on its path, it exerts a pull on the earth's oceans and forms the tides.

In parts of Acadia National Park, the rock slopes gently into the ocean. As the tide goes out, part of the sea stays behind. Water is trapped in bowl-like indentations in the rock. These shallow tide pools are a great place to explore. But be careful! The rocks are slippery. Stay far back from the waves, which can come up suddenly.

Tide pools are full of tiny plants and animals. They take refuge here from the constant pounding of the waves. Many tide pool animals live in hard shells. The common periwinkle is a tiny snail that lives in tide pools. It eats the green algae that grow on the wet rocks. Small white barnacles are animals that cling to the rocks. At low tide, they close the valve on top of their shells tight. If they did not, the delicate animals would dry out and die. When the water washes over them, their shells open. Little arms reach out to pull in food.

Life in the Tide Pools

Blue mussels secrete a kind of glue that holds them onto the rock and keeps them from washing away. Their bluish-black shells are shaped like a teardrop. Dog whelks have a spiral-shaped shell. They attack other shelled animals, such as mussels.

Whelks use their toothed tongue-like radula to drill a hole in their prey's shell.

Seaweeds, like rockweeds, kelp, and Irish moss, inhabit the pools, too. Green crabs hide under the seaweed. They have eight pointy legs and two claws. They feed on the small animals that live in the tide pools. Tide pools are fragile places that are easy to disturb. For instance, the sunscreen from your hand would seep into the water and change its composition. The park staff encourages people to look at the tide pools, but not to wade in them or touch them.[1]

→ Out On the Water

A great way to experience Acadia is to get out on the water. The views of the island are incredible. In a sea kayak, one can explore the nooks and crannies of the coastline and the harbor islands. There is no better way to view the seabirds and seals. Canoe or kayak on one of the island's many freshwater lakes. Maybe you will catch a glimpse of a beaver as it floats on its back, nibbling at a poplar branch. A loon may surface near the canoe and make its eerie call.

At the dock in Bar Harbor, there are many boat companies that take people out on the sea. A lobster boat shows how lobsters are trapped. The captain will probably show you starfish, sea cucumbers, and other sea animals also caught in the lobster trap before they are released back into the sea. A whale-watching cruise is a lot of fun. The boat locates finback or minke whales by sonar. Lucky passengers will see the whales breach and roll in the water. On all of these water tours, the boats are sure to pass puffins and seals sitting on the rocky offshore islands.

➔ RAINY DAY AT THE MUSEUM

If the weather is bad, do not despair. The weather on the coast is notorious for changing quickly. Look at it as an opportunity to spend the day enjoying a museum. At the Mount Desert Oceanarium in Bar Harbor, there is a Touch Tank with sea creatures. There are live harbor seals to view up close. And there is a lobster hatchery on site, where one can learn all about the life cycle of the lobster.

View of Acadia National Park ▷
at sunset.

The Thomas Bay marsh walk is a boardwalk through a saltwater marsh. There is a viewing tower with a telescope. It is a great spot for spying on the birds and animals that live in the marsh. At the Abbe Museum in downtown Bar Harbor, there are exhibits about the first people of Maine. See how the Wabanaki lived. Join a workshop to learn about crafts, such as intricate basket weaving. Interested in the history of people and the sea? Take a ferry to nearby Little Cranberry Island and check out the Islesford Historical Museum. The exhibits there tell the story of the area's maritime history.

⮕BASS HARBOR HEAD LIGHTHOUSE

A thick fog spreads over the ocean like a heavy blanket. A beacon of light flashes through the mist. It is the beam from a lighthouse. The flashing light helps sailors to navigate the rocky coast. Maine, with its thousands of miles of coastline, is famous for its many lighthouses. Today, the lighthouses are automated, and the Coast Guard maintains them.

In days of old, a lighthouse keeper lived in or near the lighthouse. The keeper made sure the light was kept in good working order. There are five lighthouses located near Acadia National Park. Four are offshore, on small islands. Bass Harbor Head Light, built in 1858, is the easiest lighthouse to visit. It is on the route of the Island Explorer bus.

⮕THE DRAW OF MOUNT DESERT ISLAND

Waves land with a crash on rocky ledges. Barnacles and seaweed cling to the rock for dear life. Water gurgles through the cobblestones on the beach as the tide goes out, and small crabs skitter through pools of water left behind by the tide. Dark, dense forests of pointy spruce trees grow right down to the cliffs where the ocean meets the land. Pink granite cliffs glow in the sunset. White-tailed deer bound gracefully through grassy fields. This is Acadia National Park.

Acadia is a peaceful place. In the summer, it is also a busy place, teeming with tourists. Many come to enjoy the solitude. They come to see the attractions of the island, like Sand Beach, Thunder Hole, and Cadillac Mountain, and to hike the trails and bike or horseback ride on the carriage roads. They canoe on the quiet inland ponds, or paddle kayaks out on the bays in hopes of spotting seals.

No matter why they come, most visitors leave humbled by the power of nature. Acadia is a place where the land and the sea collide. The two elements are engaged in an age-old battle, and visitors to the park have front-row seats.

Each day, the Atlantic Ocean pounds the shore. The rock is strong, but the ocean never stops. Over time, the waves carve away at the land. It has taken millions of years for the water to form the landscape of today. It is happening even now, a little bit every day. It is the raw power of nature that captivates the hearts of visitors to Acadia and brings them back to visit again and again.

		STOP						
Back	Forward	Stop	Review	Home	Explore	Favorites	History

Report Links

▶**National Park Service: Acadia National Park**
Editor's Choice The National Park Service provides a very good overview of the park.

▶*National Geographic:* **Autumn in Acadia National Park**
Editor's Choice Read this article from *National Geographic* magazine.

▶**Maps of Acadia National Park**
Editor's Choice View historical maps of Acadia National Park at this Library of Congress site.

▶**National Parks Conservation Association**
Editor's Choice This environmental nonprofit aims to protect and preserve America's national parks.

▶**Maine's Watchable Wildlife**
Editor's Choice This article explores the animals, birds, and sea life of Maine.

▶**U.S. National Parks & Monuments Travel Guide: Acadia National Park**
Editor's Choice An informational guide to the wildlife and vegetation found in the park.

▶**Abbe Museum**
This site is dedicated to celebrating the native people of Maine.

▶**Acadia**
Take a virtual tour of the special places in Acadia National Park.

▶**Acadia National Park**
Learn about the park's history and wildlife when you visit this site.

▶**Acadia National Park: At a Glance**
This is a comprehensive information guide to Acadia National Park.

▶**Acadia National Park Nature Guide**
Use this searchable database to learn about the mammals, birds, reptiles, and amphibians of the park.

▶**Bird Checklists of the United States: Acadia National Park**
Use this checklist to see what species live in the park.

▶**Building the Carriage Roads**
At this site, read about the construction of Rockefeller's carriage roads.

▶**CAMNET: Acadia National Park, Maine**
Live and archival Web cam images track air pollution in Acadia National Park.

▶**Code Red: America's Five Most Polluted National Parks**
This multi-page article looks at air pollution in our national parks.

Report Links

The Internet sites described below can be accessed at http://www.myreportlinks.com

▶**The Depths of Depression**
The Library of Congress offers this Web site about the Great Depression.

▶**Ecological Society of America (ESA)**
Conservation and preservation of ecological sites is the object of this environmental association.

▶**The Evolution of the Conservation Movement, 1850–1920**
This collection includes photographs and manuscripts about the movement to conserve nature.

▶**Friends of Acadia**
At this Web site, learn more about conservation efforts for the national park.

▶**Geology Fieldnotes: Acadia National Park**
Learn more about the geological formation and evolution of Acadia National Park.

▶**Giovanni da Verrazzano**
Read a biographical sketch of Verrazzano's life and view routes of his voyages.

▶**The Great Depression**
Learn more about the Great Depression from this detailed article.

▶**Hands on the Land: Acadia National Park**
This field classroom profiles Acadia National Park.

▶**Hudson River School**
This PBS site takes a look at the Hudson River artists.

▶**John D. Rockefeller, Junior, 1874–1960**
Read about the philanthropist's life, career, and lifelong commitment to conservation.

▶**Leave No Trace Center for Outdoor Ethics**
Find out about outdoor ethics and the principles of minimum impact on this site.

▶**The Maine Wolf Coalition**
Wolf recovery in Maine is the subject of this Web site.

▶**New Research: Peregrine Falcons Show Highest Toxic Deca Levels Ever Reported**
This site provides information about the plight of the peregrine falcon.

▶**Samuel de Champlain**
The Mariners' Museum's Web site provides details of the famous explorer's life and voyages.

▶**Woodlawn Museum**
Located near Acadia National Park, this museum helps tell the story of the park.

anomaly—A deviation from the usual. Something different or peculiar.

baleen—A filter for feeding made from keratin found in the mouths of some whales.

boreal—Of the North.

buckboard—A horse-drawn wagon with bench seats, used for sightseeing.

by-product—Something produced in addition to the principle product, or a secondary, unexpected result.

cairn—A heap or pile of stones or rocks.

carnivorous—Meat eating.

cottages—Large mansions owned by wealthy summer folk in Bar Harbor.

DDT—A chemical insecticide used after World War II to combat insects like mosquitoes that were spreading malaria, typhus, and other insect-borne human diseases.

deciduous—Only having leaves for part of the year.

fjord—A deep but narrow inlet of ocean, surrounded by cliffs.

glacial erratic—A large rock that deviates from the size and type of rock native to the area in which it rests. These rocks were carried to their new locations by glacial ice.

glacier—A thick sheet of ice that flows across the land.

granite—A type of rock found on Mount Desert Island.

hackmatack—A Maine folk name for the eastern larch tree.

inferno—A huge fire.

maritime—Having to do with the sea.

midden—A heap of clam and oyster shells left by American Indian people.

needle—The thin, pointed "leaf" of an evergreen tree.

Passamaquoddy—One of two American Indian tribes of Mount Desert Island.

Pemetic—Wabanaki name for Mount Desert Island, which means "the sloping land."

peninsula—A piece of the mainland that is bordered by water on three sides.

Penobscot—One of two American Indian tribes of Mount Desert Island.

popover—An airy pastry made of egg, butter, and flour and baked in a muffin tin.

predator—Animal that hunts other animals for food.

ration—Limited portions, as in times of war.

raze—To destroy to the ground.

scavenger—Animal that eats whatever it can find.

smallpox—A deadly disease brought to the New World by Europeans.

smog—Hazy, polluted air.

steward—A person who takes care of property for someone else.

toxin—A substance that is poisonous.

Wabanaki—"People of the dawn," a nation of American Indians from Maine and Canada.

Chapter 1. A Trip to Acadia National Park

1. Ruth Ann Hill, *Discovering Old Bar Harbor and Acadia National Park* (Camden, Maine: Down East Books, 1996), p. 123.

2. Jerry Monkman and Marcy Monkman, *Discover Acadia National Park, Second Edition: AMC Guide to the Best Hiking, Biking, Paddling* (Boston: Appalachian Mountain Club Books, 2005), pp. 9–10.

Chapter 2. History of Mount Desert Island

1. Morgan Atherton and Brian Alward, *Introduction,* 2000, <http://www.usm.maine.edu /gany/webaa/newpage1.htm> (May 30, 2007).

2. Tom Blagden, Jr., and Charles R. Tyson, Jr., *First Light: Acadia National Park and Maine's Mount Desert Island* (Englewood, Col.: Westcliffe Publishers, 2003), p. 3.

3. "The Great Dying: 1616–1619," *Abbe Museum,* n.d., <http://www.abbemuseum.org/great _dying.html> (January 12, 2007).

4. Sargent F. Collier, *Mt. Desert Island and Acadia National Park: An Informal History* (Camden, Maine: Down East Books, 1978), p. 1.

5. Russell D. Butcher, *Field Guide to Acadia National Park,* rev. ed. (New York: Taylor Trade Publishing, 2005), p. 23.

6. Samuel de Champlain, as quoted in Ruth Ann Hill, *Discovering Old Bar Harbor and Acadia National Park* (Camden, Maine: Down East Books, 1996), p. 20.

7. James Kaiser, *Acadia: The Complete Guide* (Bangor, Maine: Destination Press, 2005), p. 82.

8. Phil Patton, "The Language of Auto Emblems, *Voice: AIGA Journal of Design,* April 6, 2004, <http://journal.aiga.org/content.cfm?ContentAlias =342039> (May 30, 2007)

9. Collier, p. 44.

Chapter 3. Mount Desert Island Becomes a Park

1. "National Geographic Adventure Guide: Acadia National Park, Maine," *National Geographic Adventure Magazine,* May 2002, <http://www .nationalgeographic.com/adventure/0205/acadia. html> (August 14, 2007).

2. W. H. Sherman, "Sherman's Guide to Bar Harbor, 1892," as reprinted in Ruth Ann Hill, *Discovering Old Bar Harbor and Acadia National Park: An Unconventional History and Guide* (Camden, Maine: Down East Books, 1996), pp. 120–121.

3. James Kaiser, *Acadia: The Complete Guide* (Bangor, Maine: Destination Press, 2005), pp. 196–197.

4. Parson Anson Williams, "Fighting the Great Fire," as reprinted in Ruth Ann Hill, *Discovering Old Bar Harbor and Acadia National Park* (Camden, Maine: Down East Books, 1996), pp. 105–106.

5. Russell D. Butcher, *Field Guide to Acadia National Park,* rev. ed. (New York: Taylor Trade Publishing, 2005), p. 5.

6. Sargent F. Collier, *Mt. Desert Island and Acadia National Park: An Informal History* (Camden, Maine: Downeast Magazine, 1978), p. 92.

7. Jerry Monkman and Marcy Monkman, *Discover Acadia National Park, Second Edition: AMC Guide to the Best Hiking, Biking, Paddling* (Boston: Appalachian Mountain Club Books, 2005), p. 181.

8. "Baker Island," *Island Time: A Guide to Some of Acadia National Park's Historic Places,* (Fort Washington, Pa.: Eastern National, 1998), pp. 15–17.

Chapter 4. Plants and Animals of Acadia

1. Acadia National Park, "Peregrine Falcons," *National Park Service,* n.d., <http://www.nps.gov /acad/naturescience/peregrines.htm> (November 27, 2006).

2. "Seven Peregrine Falcons hatch at Acadia National Park," *WGME 13 News,* July 5, 2006, <http://www.wgme.com/_features/_list/DAYB_200 60705_074615_detail.html> (January 12, 2007).

3. Russell D. Butcher, *Maine Paradise: Mount Desert Island and Acadia National Park* (New York: The Viking Press, 1973), pp. 10–11.

4. James Kaiser, *Acadia: The Complete Guide* (Bangor, Maine: Destination Press, 2005), p. 70.

5. Jerry Monkman and Marcy Monkman, *Discover Acadia National Park, Second Edition: AMC Guide to the Best Hiking, Biking, Paddling* (Boston: Appalachian Mountain Club Books, 2005), pp. 86–87.

6. William H. Burt, *A Field Guide to the Mammals,* 3rd ed. (Boston: Houghton Mifflin Company, 1980), p. 243.

Chapter 5. Preserving Acadia for the Future

1. "Preservation," *Acadia: Your Complete Guide to the Park,* 24th ed., American Park Network, New York, 2006–2007, p. 39.

2. Acadia National Park Natural Resource Management, "Air Resources Program," *National Park Service,* n.d., <http://www.nps.gov/archive/acad/rm/airprog.htm> (January 12, 2007).

3. "Island Explorer Buses Use Clean Propane Fuel," *Island Explorer,* n.d., <http://www.exploreacadia.com/propane.html> (January 12, 2007).

4. "Friends of Acadia Projects," *Friends of Acadia,* April 24, 2006, <http://www.friendsofacadia.org/projects.shtml> (December 5, 2006).

5. Charles Jacobi, "Hiker Use of Mountain Summits in Acadia National Park: 2002–2003," *ANP Natural Resource Report 2003–15,* December 2003, <http://www.nps.gov/archive/acad/rm/docs/pdf/visitoruse/summit03rpt.pdf> (January 12, 2007).

6. Acadia National Park, "Caring for Cairns," *National Park Service,* n.d., <http://www.nps.gov/archive/acad/rm/docs/pdf/visitoruse/Cairns2.pdf> (January 12, 2007).

7. Charles Jacobi, "Using Signs to Reduce Visitor-Built Cairns: Gorham Mountain Trail, Acadia National Park," *ANP Natural Resource Report 2003–11,* November 2003, <http://www.nps.gov/archive/acad/rm/docs/pdf/visitoruse/Batesrpt03.pdf> (January 12, 2007).

8. Jeffrey L. Marion and Scott E. Reid, "Development of the U.S. Leave No Trace Program: An Historical Perspective," *Leave No Trace: Center for Outdoor Ethics,* January 2001, <http://www.lnt.org/about/LNTHistoryPaper.pdf> (January 12, 2007).

9. "Preservation," *Acadia: Your Complete Guide to the Park,* 24th ed. (New York: American Park Network, 2006–2007), p. 40.

10. Acadia National Park Resource Management, "Vegetation Program," *National Park Service,* n.d., <http://www.nps.gov/archive/acad/rm/vegprog .htm> (January 12, 2007).

11. Charles R. Tyson, Jr., *First Light: Acadia National Park and Maine's Mount Desert Island* (Englewood, Col.: Westcliffe Publishers, 2003), p. 59.

Chapter 6. Things to Do and See in Acadia

1. *Searching the Shore: A Guide to Tidepools in Acadia National Park,* (Fort Washington, Pa.: Eastern National, 1998).

Bily, Cynthia A., ed. *Pollution*. San Diego, Calif.: Greenhaven Press, 2006.

Brownstone, David M., and Irene M. Franck. *Frontier America*. Danbury, Conn.: Grolier, 2004.

Faber, Harold. *Samuel de Champlain, Explorer of Canada*. New York: Benchmark Books, 2005.

Hicks, Terry Allan. *Maine*. New York: Marshall Cavendish Benchmark, 2006.

Laubach, Christyna, Rene Laubach, and Charles W. G. Smith. *Raptor! A Kid's Guide to Birds of Prey*. North Adams, Mass.: Storey Publishing, 2002.

Laughlin, Rosemary. *John D. Rockefeller: Oil Baron and Philanthropist*. Greensboro, N.C.: Morgan Reynolds, 2004.

Maestro, Betsy. *Struggle for a Continent: The French and Indian Wars: 1689–1763*. New York: HarperCollins, 2000.

Petersen, David, and Christine Petersen. *The Atlantic Ocean*. New York: Children's Press, 2001.

Vogel, Carole Garbuny. *Ocean Wildlife (The Restless Sea)*. New York: Franklin Watts, 2003.

Yanuchi, Jeff, and Lori Yanuchi. *Ranger Trails: Jobs of Adventure in America's Parks*. Healy, Ala.: Ridge Rock Press, 2005.